# NOTE TO SELF:

## a collection of 99 life lessons

BRYAN WEMPEN

INHERITANCE PRESS

INHER|TANCE
P R E S S

Published by Inheritance Press LLC
Lake Mary, Florida 32746
www.inheritancepress.com

Cover image courtesy of Michella Estrada
Bio photo by Steph Grant
Jacket design by Tom Morse-Brown

Library of Congress Control Number: 2015939319

ISBN: 978-0-9823859-6-8

Printed in the United States of America

*This book is dedicated to Michella. I wouldn't have figured this out without you. Thank you.*

*A special thanks to my friends who shared:*
Jason Seiden, Michella Estrada, Doug Shaw, Lindsey Clark-Aguilar, Shela Tarwater, Randy Roberts, Angela Maiers, Kirstie Johnson, Laurie Ruettiman, Jay Kuhns, Heather Bussing, Mike Vandervort.

*An extra-special thanks my super-star team who got this done:*
Kirstie Johnson, Editor
Monique Donahue, Publisher

*Lastly, I appreciate all those who were part of me putting pieces of the puzzle in place:*
Cat Carlos, Ben Brooks, Chris Havrilla, Teela Jackson, Jenny DeVaughn, Heather Bussing, John Sumser, Randy Roberts, Shela Tarwater, Mia Pearl Leighty, Kirstie Johnson, William Tincup, Nisha Raghavan, Rosemary Sumner, Ally & Anna Reynolds, Chris Wright and Donna Wempen (Mom), LeRoy Wempen (Dad), Diana Wempen Connell (Sis), Barb Stever (Mother).

# Contents

# Foreword

A YEAR AGO, I WAS PREPARING A presentation to 800 high school students to tell them that they could change the world. A week before the event, it expanded to all 6,000 students in the district. Desperate to supplement my staff, I invited scores of people in my network to fly across the country to spend two days working with students, on a pro bono basis. Needless to say, I got very few responses. But there standing next to me as the event began was Bryan Wempen, who then did a remarkable job helping me set the tone and then meeting with countless groups of students over the next two days. Bryan is compassionate, reflective, and yet action-oriented, and I am blessed to call him a friend.

Through this series of lessons, he shares from his heart and soul the many lessons he has learned along the way to becoming the extraordinary person that he is. I am honored that he invited me to contribute to this remarkable collection of wisdom. No matter your reason for reading this book, the lessons shared will make you a more compassionate, humble and centered person.

—*Angela Maiers*

# Introduction

WITH HELP AND MY OWN WILLINGNESS, I've finally opened myself up to listen and discover myself. Thank you to so many who inspire and support me.

> "Your visions will become clear only when you can look into your own heart. Who looks outside, dreams; who looks inside, awakes."
>
> —C.G. JUNG

Life is an adventure, which is what I recommit to everyday. I've definitely not always enjoyed my life this way. Laughing every single day is mandatory, damn it—life is funny. I made a choice early in this process to share what I've learned by referencing my experiences. I'm sure that some people won't agree with my perspective or maybe identify with a story, which is just fine. My goal is to get you thinking and talking about some important things.

I've found that some parts of the book can seem a little heavy and have a darker mood, nevertheless the topics are serious but there is no reason that laughter shouldn't be found. I get the privilege of joking around and laughing with people at meetings who are working hard to save their own lives. Life is short, I laugh about as much as I can as often as I can.

I attribute some of my ability to laugh-a-lot and maintain a sense of humor to my parents, family and friends growing up who seemed to find humor in life. None of us are perfect but hopefully we can now laugh about that too.

The book is filled with the lessons I've found to be important to managing very human ups, downs and ups. My learning to pay attention to the lessons I'm presented with in life, as tough as they can be, it's all part of who I will be in the future. Not until my early 40's did I start to find a voice of who I was and could be.

Several years ago I was unhappy and would invest significant amounts of time and energy into a facade, a mask of what was going on internally with me. It was a carnival ride of emotions and thoughts. I was completely lacking in an ability to process much of anything dealing with mind, body and soul. It's quite the hamster cage to make decisions and manage life from fear, insecurity and self-centeredness.

As my friend says in his keynote talks, "I was living with no authenticity."

Most of the outside world would probably say that I was happy, confident and fairly successful. The outside was a lie, the inside a mess and rather empty. I was successful enough but unhappy and unfulfilled. At 40 years old my painful, honest and joyful new chapter started with being willing to be honest with myself and starting to self-reflect. The self-awareness didn't start right away; most people aren't able to flip the switch to "fixed" when these life-changing shifts happen. It's definitely a process filled with awkwardness and imperfection, but it's still a process that takes time. My starting line for this new phase of life is definitely not unique; it rose out of pain that has been piled up until I reached my limit. This is the day I stopped drinking.

The new journey started with my own Note-to-Self: "I can't continue living this way, something has to change." I was so unhappy I couldn't breath and I didn't know what the heck to do.

Brief story: I'm in Chicago riding to the airport in the back of a cab leaving an HR unConference hung-over, sick and truly lost. I just wanted to disappear, be lost for a while. This was an intersection where my spirit and I really connected for the first time. I was physically tired, spiritually empty and emotionally bankrupt.

As the tears started, my world felt small and I felt smaller and very alone: the feeling I battled most of my life. The loneliness and isolation feeling was real to me, albeit self-imposed and a reminder to myself that my feelings aren't facts. Was I able to talk to people, share my feelings? No, my world was about me not being comfortable with most anything, or myself, so I chased ways to change how I felt much. Over the years, self-medicating with alcohol and food and working all the time were my way to deal with the chaos. I was void of healthy coping skills, healthy ways to process my feelings; they just weren't developed in my earlier years and absolutely absent as an adult.

My career has been about promoting myself to back up my actions. High-performer with not much of a life, work 100 hours, again work was how I dealt with my uneasiness. In looking back it's amazing that I've been professionally as successful as I've been. Being a successful, professional entrepreneur is the dream I have been chasing, I have partially accomplished this some years and missed the mark other years—I guess this by itself is the typical entrepreneurial story. It was my personal chaos that was the biggest driver in the backdrop of all that I was doing. We're now back at the interaction I'd mentioned, a crossroads of my decision to get help and get healthier—make things real and honest. This process allowed me to quit carrying around the guilt, shame, fear, self-hatred and insecurity that consumed so many years. I was finally able to see what being free of this looked like.

I stopped drinking on May 9, 2010 and realized something was terribly wrong with my life and something had to change. For some reason doing this all alone was never something I considered, I felt I couldn't do it alone. This was my "Note to Self" day. This is what many people call my emotional and spiritual bottom. Yes, I could have gone lower—some really amazing people do— and never come back, but I didn't for whatever reason.

This was my starting point: my willingness where I was asking for help, going to any lengths to change my life. Since that point, I consistently ask for help and guidance and have gained knowledge and experience that keeps me sane, sober and serving a greater purpose. When I want a reference point for something important, I acknowledge it by saying it and writing it down. I use these life lessons on my daily journey; my serenity depends on it. My hope is these lessons, shared by friends and myself, will give anyone who reads them additional perspectives on life to think about. My experience is that life can change if willingness is a priority, and life can be a lot better.

I've made incredible progress physically, emotionally and spiritually (mind, body and soul) since the day my life changed. Sharing this collection of life lessons will hopefully help me continue to grow, evolve and be a reference point for others.

## Chapter 1

# Progress not Perfection

I'VE FELT THESE THREE LITTLE WORDS offer comfort and clarity so many times. It's nice to have sayings to bridge sets of feelings, frustrations, humor and especially sadness. I use many of these little sayings with a goal of not allowing the awesome world and myself to be so serious. Perfection is impossible to achieve so I ask myself why do many others and I set and measure progress to perfect-like goals. I'm able to achieve progress every single day. I refer to these lessons all the time; I feel I'd be lost again without their guidance.

## Lesson 1: Don't abandon myself. I'm awesome.

The challenge was not how to avoid abandoning myself, but being completely clueless on knowing a starting point to find myself. There was no starting point until this point was right in front of me. I didn't know or like who I was and I was truly lost.

When I didn't understand I was looking for a starting line, it was impossible to find a path to the start; the lack of vision and awareness was genuinely an emotional and spiritual desert and I was wandering. I felt disconnected with people, places and things.

It feels like you're wandering and drifting around. Some people never find a starting line, and I feel bad for them. It's a life of wandering and I didn't want that. That just feels like a life wasted.

I didn't want to fade away to the end. I wanted more. My starting point was a point where unhappiness became unbearable. I was ready to do whatever it takes to change where I was at then. That day was May 9, 2010.

I've discovered something every day since then about who I am and what I want to be. I've found I'm a decent person and am able to give myself permission to be human, which means successes and failures. I work daily to make progress. It's a priority to forgive myself when I don't make much progress, even when I fall backwards in life. Be kind to yourself today.

## Lesson 2: We're all damaged in some way. Everyone's got something.

The kid in the wheelchair wears his wheels where everyone can see it. So does the smoking hot blonde, if you know how to spot insecurity behind a smile. The quiet girl in the corner is afraid she's a freak, and the guy with it all figured out? He's living off his wife's largess.

The older I get, the less I judge. How would I know what it's like to carry your burden around every day? When I was younger, judgment came easier, because the world looked easier than it is. But the more I discovered those hidden burdens, the more I came to see the handcuffs people wrestle with—the scars, the conditioning, the damage—and the harder it became for me to judge them.

Everyone's got something. We're all damaged in some way.

That's what unites us and makes us whole. My friend Jason Seiden shared this lesson.

## Lesson 3: I'm alone and that's all right.

*"When you are lonely, you are looking for someone or something to fill your time, to fill the void in your schedule and to fill a void in your heart. Alone is a positive state of mind, a very fulfilling place to be. It is a state where you are always and constantly delighted in yourself."*

—INDIA HOPE, MINDBODYGREEN.COM

The feeling of being lonely and alone comes in many types, shapes and feelings; I absolutely understand and empathize with all of them. At times being alone has been overwhelming, and when I felt this emotion it resembled physical pain but it wasn't physical pain—it was just being uncomfortable with myself. Basically I wasn't comfortable being alone with myself. I figured out this had to change to be happier.

We all have experienced both loneliness and hopefully aloneness in our life. This awareness about these feelings forced me to examine what I call my physical, emotional and spiritual fitness; others refer to this as mind, body and soul.

These three things have become my cornerstone for living my life. After some self-awareness work I started to communicate better with myself about what loneliness and aloneness meant. My little internal dialog about this subsided to be not so dramatic about being alone because it's ok. Alone tends to be where I find growth and clarity; this was a huge realization for me.

What I've found is I have to stay as centered as possible. When balance happens across my three cornerstones I don't feel alone and the world feels big and infinite, which is a good thing. When I neglect any of these areas and get out of balance—i.e. out-of-whack—for very long, the world gets small quickly because I'm collapsing into a chaotic limited self. I remind myself daily to work on the tools I need to stay balanced.

## Lesson 4: Aloneness and loneliness are simply complex feelings.

Loneliness is about me, not anyone else, but that sure doesn't make it feel any better when it's happening. Loneliness can feel like a void or gap in happiness, but it's more about the gap in my growth. Sure doesn't feel great but I grow. It's a shift from having external conversations to feel complete, to having inward conversations instead. Without this it's like I'm missing something, an ingredient for the recipe of complete happiness.

The real goal is being able to be satisfied while being alone. This is being quiet so inside I can explore, discover and fully engage. Being able to grow that intimate relationship with "self" has given me more insight into my sanity and being happy than most anything else. Which begs the question—if I know that "aloneness" is fulfilling, then why does it feel so bad when it happens at times? My conclusion is that I've got more work to do on myself; it's a great indicator of opportunities for me to grow.

## Lesson 5: Read whatever you want, read often.

I am someone who has gone through wild up and down swings with how much I read. There is a magic formula for me that works for me to read more often. It's thinking about what I should read for business and then mixing that up with pleasure reading. The pleasure readings are things that catch and hold my interest, such as history, biographies, magazines and fiction.

Attention can drift and wander like many, so I address this by reading multiple books at one time, which holds my interest. I have no clue if there is a better way or not to read. I figured the key was to just keep reading something. It's all right to be completely abstract in my consumption of information: bite size or full-on buffet-style, let-the-pants-out type reading. My mind feels better and I work better when I read new information constantly. This realization was the genesis to jump back into reading so often.

Technology has played an important role in the frequency of when I pick up a book. I've found I read quicker and retain more information when not reading the traditional book. I learned to embrace what works for me; when I read with my Kindle on my iPhone and iPad, the digital experience works for me. I still love the feel and experience of traditional books, but I read better and more often with my technology. Know myself, Know thyself and thank you Kindle.

## Lesson 6: I depend on you; I'm not dependent on you.

Life is funny when I start trying to explain using my thoughts and words about what I am feeling and my emotions. I've worked through my stuff with co-dependency. It was one of the most significant breakthroughs of my life. My work on dependency started with learning the difference—the definition of being interdependent versus a raging co-dependent.

Trust is the cornerstone for me when I depend on someone. Completely depending on someone was a gigantic realization that it could happen. Once this happened, the cascading effect included being able to articulate how I felt about several important relationships in my life. This personal growth spurt happened with tons of self-reflection and self-awareness—deep and really hard work. I feel it also doesn't stop; I work on making progress not perfection.

My enlightenment all started with my willingness to admit I had some issues and needed to do some work. Then talking with those who could offer great perspective and help me help myself.

## Lesson 7: Balance is the key.

Who knew that staying balanced takes a lot of work? I sure as heck didn't until my journey of self-awareness started. But think about it—most people don't just jump on a tight rope and walk across a raging river with confidence and balance.

Balance in all parts of my life really does take work, practice and commitment to grow and improve. I work on balancing three main areas: physical, emotional and spiritual fitness. When I distribute the work equally on the three areas, life works pretty well. When I get out of balance it can be bumpy or even rough at times. It's like a tire that gets out of balance; I feel it a little at first, then hang-on when it goes way out of balance. Things can get rough until I figure out the problem. Then I start working on the solution. What does my solution look like?

## Lesson 8: Me, myself and I are crowded.

Chatter...chatter...chatter. My mind at times will not stop, seriously the inner-dialog running wild until I focus and say "stop it" to my mind. I'm not alone; I know many people I've spoken with who have the loop of self-conversation going on in their mind. Mine is chaotic, usually negative and damn well doesn't make me feel joyous and free.

I met a guy years ago that referred to it as his "committee" meeting in his head—such an appropriate description. I've found it clogs and occupies space that the positive narrative would otherwise occupy, the ones that come from my peaceful and balanced times. We only have so much room; the negative/self-deprecating/self-pity/self-hating script that plays out at times limits growth and overall fitness.

When I practice, prioritize and figure out ways to get out of "self" even only for a single moment, I'm productive—less bumps in the road. My routine is to start and end my day with a moment of quiet. I feel happier and way more present when I am following my routine. It could be "stopping my committee" by being of service to others. You can also: meditate, read, pray, chant, write, breathe, stretch, walk, run, bike, paint, sew, draw, cook, watch a movie, call a friend, call a family member, call a sponsor and many more. I felt life got better when I learned to take my emotional and spiritual breaks. Might take one right now, how about you?

## Lesson 9: Breathe in and out.

I was told something that was shocking that I needed to be told—breathe. Then being someone who works on self-awareness daily, I was told something else more surprising—breathe in and out, it works better that way. What is the deal; don't I pay attention to my basic needs? No, it's more about reacting to life versus responding. When I am balanced and focused on listening to the universe, I naturally breathe in and out. This is what I call responding to life. When I'm not in a balanced place I find myself not breathing so effortlessly. This I call reacting to life.

About balance, a universe always in balance from small to the largest situations, I'm guessing will always be a debate for human beings. Listening to myself breathe is the universe to me, without it no balance happens. I find myself reminding myself that balance is part of understanding and learning. All that being said, learning to breathe was way more complicated and beneficial that I ever imagined. This area has taken me more work to appreciate, understand and put into action.

It seems so basic—how many ways can you breathe? But I remember in sports as a kid, I learned how to breathe during a workout, intense play and extended periods of physical stress. I started to hear the words, "remember to breathe." Add oxygen into my body with frequency and a certain cadence of breathing and good things happen. Take a moment to look up the practice—tonglen meditation; it's been very helpful for me.

*"A mind at ease has an easy breath."*

—BRYAN WEMPEN

## Lesson 10: Belief systems aren't perfect or permanent, they are you.

I believe I start out with a belief system that I inherited from my family. And as I move through life, I tend to gather friends and mates in my life who hold similar beliefs. But as I move out from my inner circle, I find people whose beliefs differ from my own. I enjoy meeting people with differing beliefs because the diversity of thought opens me up to see things differently. But sometimes, this difference can also be a source of conflict.

So, what happens when you have one of these encounters and your belief systems are shaken? I see that beliefs, as we mature, are based on our perceptions of experiences. As you encounter new experiences, do you shift your belief systems and incorporate the new points of view or do you end the relationship?

Could it be that beliefs are like a door or an avenue between people to explore? Could they be there to put perspective between you and the world?

I think beliefs are malleable like clay or putty; you can try them on and take them off, and repeat until you find what works best for you. Each situation you face gives you a chance to sort and sift and find yourself again in this world. Do you want to feel safe or do you want to explore? Your values underneath your beliefs will guide your way. My friend Kirstie Johnson shared this lesson.

## Lesson 11: Find something to believe in that's bigger than myself.

Living started again that day, 5-9-10. It was the first day I wanted to change how I felt by discovery and self-awareness versus drinking. It started by surrendering to something bigger than myself for help. That something bigger than myself was undefined—not tangible, I couldn't see it or hear it—but I was the point I wanted to believe.

They happened at this specific moment, why I don't understand or need to understand. There was a point where I needed to grasp on to something because I felt like I had nothing. The hopelessness had become heavy, easing this weight all started with my admitting I had a problem and I needed help. Willingness.

Once I admitted to myself and something greater than myself that I couldn't do life any longer without help, this opened up my spirit, I was willing to listen to life and try this living thing.

## Lesson 12: The more good things I believe.

Positive thoughts can't be walked away from and underestimated on how they will impact life. I enjoy focusing on the positive; in a way that embraces challenges and negative feelings I'm dealing with. It actually addresses what is going on in my mind, body and soul when I believe in myself.

Embracing self-awareness and discovery is finding out why I think the way I do, good and bad. It becomes less negative and more positive over time; it lessens time spent in those darker places. Life is about balance. The frequency and severity will lessen I promise; it did for me with lots of work. I've learned to opt in quicker and with more confidence for things of value to me. I opt out of those things that don't bring value.

## Lesson 13: Be brave. Choose to matter.

Mattering is a choice. We choose to matter, and we choose to recognize that others matter. This sounds easy. Of course everyone matters. But choosing to matter is an intentional act. It requires us to own our genius.

Firstly, it requires that you identify what your genius is and proclaim it. For instance, "I am a connector; I bring people together." Or maybe, "I am a leader; I show others the way."

Secondly, it requires that you identify where your genius is needed. There are thousands of children that need teaching, streets that need sweeping, and cars that need building—but there is a specific place where you are needed.

Lastly, choosing to matter requires that you notice the genius around you and leverage it for collective good. Every accomplishment is in some way a partnership. Seeing the genius around you is essential to making real the changes that matter to you.

Of the 21st-century skills you can learn, an ability to recognize and pursue what matters most to you may be the most important. It guides the focus of all our talents. It is imperative that this process of mattering integrates into your daily life. With it, your capacity to spur change is boundless. My friend Angela Maiers shared this lesson.

## Chapter 2

# The Mirror

Looking in the mirror is powerful if we open more than our eyes. We're all mirrors of what we do and don't like, who we want to be and who we are. I'm committed to open my mind, body and spirit to my truth every chance I get. I feel the opportunity I've been presented with everyday is a great responsibility—one of the reasons why I'm sharing the lessons. I'm inspired by what has been learned by myself and my friends.

I'm committed to physical, emotional and spiritual growth until the very end of life. Those are very broad goals, so I'm going to break it down: today I'm doing the next right thing, sharing these lessons with you and a smile with another human being. Tomorrow when I look in the mirror, I will use what I learned from today.

### Lesson 14: If nothing changes, nothing changes.

What would life be like if I could do nothing different and my life just changed, improved in the way I wanted—literally followed my perfect script. It means I would increase physical endurance without exercising; gain experience without working on a project. Not to my surprise, the pursuit of rainbows and unicorns just doesn't work that way. I had said to myself, "something has to change for the outcome to change." Change my pattern, change my behavior, and change the way I think, shake it up, and zag a bit, whatever it takes to positively make a change in my life. That is how it works for me. I could also change nothing, and then nothing would change. I make these choices every single day, it's called living my life the best I can.

## Lesson 15: Healthy ways to change how I feel.

Not a new story that food, alcohol, sex, drugs, tobacco, exercise, shopping, co-dependency, gambling and workaholism are some of the ways people cope with what life sends our way.

These are not the healthiest of ways I used to change how I felt. Some of these things, in small socializing amounts, can be just fine.

For many, these tendencies are the wall that keeps everyone away from real issues that need to be coped with. My coping tools kept me from working on myself; I had so many walls up that prevented a path to physical, emotional and spiritual fitness and health. Life started to change when I started to address the fear, pain, and gaps in my coping skills and how I was changing how I felt. That day was a start for me; I started and stopped what was going on inside me.

This allowed me to start to deal with the more significant issues that I'd avoided with outside means for years, for a lifetime I suppose if I'm being completely honest.

Yes, this is difficult, it takes work daily—I have to be humble and be grateful every day. By no means is anything I will do be a "super-pill" that fixes everything forever. This is my starting point to managing life on life's terms.

## Lesson 16: It's never too late to change my mind.

Life is not so cut and dried most of the time for me, life is just a crazy shade of gray. I've found it challenging to change emotional directions, go against the momentum of my own damn decisions. I've discovered when I become uncomfortable I hesitate then have to force myself to ask myself questions about what is going on. Quite the process for changing my mind on something, but at least now that I know this is a challenge for me, talking it through always helps.

As I examine how I evaluate and think about things I discover when I should stop and start thoughts. For me, fear of change can be rooted in many things—a fear of the past repeating itself and fear of unknown outcomes. Most people are able to overcome a fear of failure and a fear of the unknown by typically attempting what they fear. Small steps on this can work; no need to jump out of an airplane because you fear parachutes, unless you really want fly.

It's incredibly liberating and powerful when I am able to voice my opinion or change my mind and not feel bad about it. All the unaddressed and undiscovered patterns from the past that keep me from making the best decisions about my life can be left behind with all this work I've done and will do in the future. If I get to a core issue I can address and overcome the fear, heal the scar and keep growing in a healthy way. We all can change our minds, there shouldn't be a scorecard and most of the time there isn't.

## Lesson 17: I don't wanna be me.

Have you ever taken a step back from your current role and compared it to what you thought you would be doing at this point? What were you expecting? Was it a certain title...or salary...or span of control? How close are you to achieving that vision?

For many, that vision is a cruel reminder of what their career is not. That can really hurt.

Wallow. When those feelings get churned up we often try to suppress them as quickly as possible. After all, we're professionals! Being under control is a hallmark of our leadership skill set. Except the suppression strategy is not real. Feeling disappointment, frustration, and even some bitterness is normal. Don't bury those feelings and please don't disregard them in some sort of artificial cleansing exercise.

Wallow in the pain. Let it consume you. Allow your honest feelings to flow hard through your mind and body. Experience those raw emotions...and feel the pain.

And only then, begin to release them.

Allowing yourself to feel alive, even when it is painful, actually turns out to be quite empowering. As counterintuitive as that may sound, life has a way of using our frustrations and disappointments as fuel to bring the future into greater focus.

Get Moving. Once your self-inflicted pain session is complete it is time for action. Get yourself organized. Start a list of what you want, now. Don't sell yourself short as you document what it is you really want. Put it all down on paper (or Wunderlist if you've committed to a digital life like me).

This list...regardless of how long, is your new beginning. You don't have to achieve anything on your list today, but you absolutely need to acknowledge that it exists. Your new plan has just been born. Give yourself credit for starting. Nothing keeps disappointment and bitterness going strong more than inaction. So take action!

How About You? Titles..money...power, all may have a role to play in your plan. However, being someone other than you makes no sense, so stop the comparisons and focus on your list. Organize it, take small steps, and start being the real you. After all, it's a lot more satisfying to say "I Wanna Be Me!" Don't you think? My friend Jay Kuhns shared this lesson.

## Lesson 18: I can't give away my power of choice to feel good and bad.

By definition "power" is:
1. The ability to do something or act in a particular way, especially as a faculty or quality.
2. The capacity or ability to direct or influence the behavior of others or the course of events.
3. Physical strength and force exerted by something or someone.

Do we really have any power over anything? It's an age-old question asked, pondered and philosophized. Power is one of the terms which relies on context for it to land in the appropriate place in what I do, say and feel. When I'm trying to be something or someone I'm not, then I've given away my power of choice to external force for validation. That is where I get messed up; that searching for outside validation is hollow and fleeting. It's like a donut, dripping with sugar and fried in something—the first bite is magical, but that's not real because it won't continue to taste good to me soon enough.

My ability to feel good or bad has to be my choice, just as eating vegan or not is my choice. I can't give that to someone or something else because I end up feeling nothing, empty and still wanting. When I allow something other than my power-of-choice to control my emotions, I have given away my power. Don't do it, it sucks. It feels infinitely liberating to have that power and be friends with it.

## Lesson 19: Get comfortable in my own skin.

Looking in the mirror," as a phrase, has slowly evolved into a mantra for me. It's one of my cornerstones for discovery, self-awareness and growth. My journey has many starts and stops, at times with not a clue where the mirror is even located or what the hell I'm looking at; that is being honest with myself. What I've learned about the "mirror" is that it doesn't lie; it's a self-reflection of inner-self—what others can not see.

There are times I feel strong, and I've discovered this feeling is good if I manage it, or it could turn into a negative because it becomes more ego than strength. When I'm more honest in my introspection of self, more objective and use healthy reference points to process "why" I'm feeling things, then I have more clarity.

Enlightenment leads to allowing myself to be a work in progress, make mistakes, start and stop many times but always be self-aware and willing to change and grow. I won't always have an answer at the start of a feeling but I'm willing and open to find it;

that is growth for me. Finding myself at ease and peace during great and tough times as I reflect in that figurative mirror is "being comfortable in my own skin."

## Lesson 20: Sore muscles are good.

There was this one time; I could barely lift myself out of my chair. This phrase has been uttered by myself and others many, many times three days into a new workout plan. Muscle memory is doing something over and over again until it makes sense without so much management.

When my muscles are sore, there is activity. I'm discovering something new or maybe finding something old—soreness can happen emotionally, spiritually or physically. The negative energy is stored in all sorts of places; figuring out how to relax the soreness in whatever form eases my stress.

My example: I'm experiencing sore legs due to starting an eight week training program. I planned it out and felt I was easing into the workout routine. Well the outcome was I'm ridiculously sore and have learned a lesson about where to start and stop my activity. If sore is good then I was great.

I started to wonder how long before I'm able to function again with less pain? Good question. Much like the emotional and spiritual workout this means I was not aligned on what activity I thought I could sustain. In reflection this soreness is exactly what I needed despite my plan.

My plan needed work; I needed to change my path just like other facets of my life. I said "self," it's time to regroup, make adjustments and figure out a new workout plan. It was a great example of being "present" versus projecting who I should be relative to fitness. I am working back to being more fit, only doing it slower and with more patience. Lessons for me happen all day long, many of which guarantee becoming sore for a while. It's part of my growth—so I now expect it.

## Lesson 21: Connectedness. It starts within.

There is always a little piece of each one of us that feels different, separate, and even alone. Sometimes we even want or need to be this way. And the truth is, we deeply yearn for connection—to love and be loved—to give and to receive unconditionally. The dichotomy of this truth has tugged at my heartstrings for as long as I can remember. I now know that there was a point in my history that created this feeling of disconnection. To me, connectedness is a state of being that I had forgotten along the way.

When I made the decision to turn inward, I witnessed those vulnerable places inside of me that were battered and broken that sought separateness. Then, awareness of my desire to experience true connection enveloped me. And as much as I wanted it, I also feared it. Through consistent stillness, inward reflection, prayer and contemplation, I now know that there is nothing to be afraid of. There is nothing in the universe that is independent. We are connected to each other and all things living. This lesson shared by my friend Shela Tarwater.

## Lesson 22: Consistent in thought.

Last week I had a conversation that has stuck in my mind. I met an individual and we were speaking about life experiences and in particular our divorces. I said that I get along with my former spouse and it is a very conscious effort. We still work together on family matters and our main concern is our children, albeit now in their 20s. From my side there is no ill will. I very much cared for him, and never want to negate that time in our lives, much less our children's. I relayed my thoughts to the individual and he said, "That is very adult of you."

The reply reminded me of why I aspire to be consistent in thought. When I have a belief or viewpoint on how I want to live my life, I carry it through my life in as many ways as possible. In this case, if I have the desire for my former spouse to respect and care about me, I should be consistent in thought and offer that to him first. My friend Michella Estrada shared this lesson.

## Lesson 23: Letting go takes a lot of courage.

I don't know how to be uncomfortable. Do I embrace this by letting go of what is comfortable? It sounds so simple, but it isn't. It's very much a stop and a starting point but there is nothing simple about it. I feel even starting this process is empowering because it felt so foreign.

Then came the rest of the feelings with letting go: a feeling of loss that comes with any type of change. Yes, there are degrees of holy shit this is heavy. Next, a feeling of anger—I was angry with everyone involved but really was angry with myself for getting to this place. What changed with time and work on self-awareness was my feelings were more about "me" than the actual loss. I started second guessing everything because everything was based on what felt easier to deal with.

But finally there was a point where the comfortable place became an unfulfilling abyss, a void: I decided this was not what I wanted any longer. That point is when a great thing happens, my pain zeros in clarity and I move forward in life.

Wish someone would have told me ghost patterns show up even years later but they are not the facts. They are just feelings to figure out and deal with. Finding courage to face my feelings, authentic self, and where I'm at today is my goal-for today. Again, all about moving forward.

> *"Letting go for me has become trusting in the process that there's a net of the universe that catches and carries me vs. me needing to control the details. It's more like becoming comfortable with the free fall."*
>
> —KIRSTIE JOHNSON

## Lesson 24: Good at being terrified.

A lawyer I worked with told me he was blown away because I wasn't afraid of anything. I had no idea what he was talking about. I'm scared of everything. I just don't let it interfere with what I want to do.

Fear is not something to fight, overcome, ignore, hide from, or defeat. It's not a weakness. Fear is good stuff. It protects us, gives us important information, and motivates us.

The trouble starts when we believe it's too hard, people will think we're stupid, or I'm just not good enough. When everything is too scary, we shut down and make our world small so we can control it. We close our minds and our hearts to anything new or different.

That's why fear is the root of discrimination and resistance to change. It manifests in arrogance, power plays, violence, backbiting, control issues, withdrawal, and pretty much anything that makes other people unpleasant to be around. I tried to fight fear especially at work where I felt I had more control over myself—I tried to overcome it. I just ended up completely focused on how scared I was, which paralyzed me. Also, the scotch it took to silence it wasn't worth the consequences.

So I've learned to just invite fear along for the ride. I give it a little attention, tell it some jokes, and ask it, very nicely, to stay in the backseat. When the fear is insistent, I listen to what it's trying to tell me. But I don't believe everything I feel or think when I'm scared. And I try not to make big decisions out of fear (or anger).

Usually, it's just that I'm worried about the outcome. I'm anxious about uncertainty.

Yet, most things are uncertain, almost all the time. And that is neither a good nor a bad thing. It's just how it is. So instead of getting caught in the crisis, or drama, or insecurity, now I notice it. And then remember that I'm really good at terrified. My friend Heather Bussing shared this lesson.

## Lesson 25: There is nothing more daunting than the idea of taking a leap or rather taking a risk.

The word "risk" may be four letters, but it's very definition strikes a bit of fear in me: "a hazard or dangerous chance." Let's be honest: why on earth would anyone choose to take a dangerous chance when we can play it safe, right? It's almost rhetorical.

But what if…What if the greatest danger of all is playing it safe, staying on the sidelines of life, and never taking a leap of faith?

As humans, each of us have dreams + desires for the future. However, often, we allow the enormity of the dream or the reality of our current circumstances to keep us sitting on the sidelines of life. We come up with a million and one reasons why what we want the most in life can never come true. So we sit still, paralyzed, and instead of experiencing everything that life has to offer us, we experience nothing.

I have this theory: Life is a lot like crossing a raging river.

To get from one side of the river to the other you have to take a leap. You have to find that first rock to step on, then from there find other stones or fallen trees to be your stepping stones to get across the river. But with each step, you take a leap, whether big or small. At some points while crossing the river, your toes may get wet, and the rocks may be slippery and you may fall, but you get back up and take another leap. Eventually, the combination of your steps leads you across the raging river. Your leaps across the river not only lead you to your destination, but give you something that can never be replaced or bought: beautiful experiences + stories.

This is life.

Taking a leap, taking a risk—when you break it down to little daily decisions, it doesn't seem as daunting. Yes, sometimes it is a gamble because you don't know the outcome, but focus on the possibilities! When you begin to focus on the extravagant possibilities that come with your risk, the risk begins to seem like a daring opportunity instead of a "dangerous chance." Your decision to take a risk will take you on the most wild + brilliant journey of life. A life that could never be attained by sitting still paralyzed by fear, but a life that is full of beautiful unexpected experiences.

My challenge to you is this: May you never be afraid to take a leap, knowing that it could lead to the life that you have always dreamed of. May your eyes be opened to the array of possibilities, instead of the dangers. Last but not least, may you never fear the idea of taking a risk but instead may the fear of walking through life paralyzed be the very thing that propels you to take a leap of faith. My friend Lindsey Clark-Aguilar shared this lesson.

## Chapter 3

# Feel Your Feelings

A s I'm taught more about myself in my personal evolution, a wonderful thing happened: I figured out that I am totally allowed and able to be in the middle of my own emotions. I've found this to be an excellent process for managing my life; it's also great therapy to work through the challenges, opportunities, tears and laughs, which make ones life. These lessons are shared to offer "food-for-thought" versus making you hangry*. Not sure that is as funny a sentence as I feel it is but oh well, it's staying in the book.

*Hangry = hungry + angry.

## Lesson 26: Eat, breathe, and feel. Repeat.

It made sense to adopt and embrace several key cornerstones in my life that support my serenity and the growth of my physical, emotional and spiritual fitness. My daily intentional practice of purposeful eating, intentional breathing (in with the negative, then pushing out with the positive) and feeling my feelings are all great. These cornerstones are my new and redefined reality and my foundation. I focus on feeding and caring for them on a daily basis.

It's easy not to give them attention and love but I choose to make that a priority.

When I do invest and focus on these important areas, they make my life more enjoyable and richer to live and enjoy. It's about my balance and consistent progress with all three.

## Lesson 27: Don't apologize for how you feel.

When I reflect back to how I used to process and convey my feelings; the pattern was to seek out the courage to say how I'm really feeling—then very quickly retreat and offer an apology for what I just shared. It was a horrible cycle.

A good friend noticed my pattern and thank goodness was honest with me and said I should stop apologizing for sharing what I'm feeling. Sharing what is going on with yourself is who you are at that moment, it's you. I'm definitely a work in progress as I occasionally catch myself still apologizing for conveying my feelings, but at least I know I'm doing it and learn from the situation. I see many other people doing this and I feel you and I are worth sharing our feelings. Seizing the opportunity to correct my slip out loud and say: No I'm not sorry, for how I feel is who I want to be.

## Lesson 28: No one has the right.

Dr. Polly is someone from my past, really just a name and one sentence of wisdom. The sentence was: "No one has the right to make you feel bad." I will remember that for the rest of my life.

This quote was actually shared with me at a difficult time for a friend. They shared it with me as they went through their self-awareness and self-discovery phase of life. I've revisited and shared those words many times over the years. The gist of what I take away from it would be: NO person has the right to hurt anyone, purposefully, and make him or her feel bad.

Hurtful comments, malicious actions, berating and bullying are all actions that happen daily to people but shouldn't. You matter and deserve better. These types of actions are unkind not compassionate and should not be tolerated. If you're tolerating this and feeling bad, then ask yourself why. Why am I allowing this to happen to myself? Skills to learn: an ability to create a boundary and communicate why it's not acceptable. This was a skill I learned after I stopped drinking; it was a harder skill for me to learn but also one of the most significant.

I have to look at my part in the interaction. Why am I interacting with this person? He or she is a complete asshole, unkind and narcissistic. Sounds nice, right? Hell no! This is a lesson I've thought about many times and shared it with many others.

## Lesson 29: What someone else is feeling.

Self-centeredness can be as obvious as: I'm more important than you so I'm always going to be late. My time is worth more than yours. No one will ever say that to me, but that is the outcome of his or her actions. Self-centeredness can be very subtle yet more damaging and powerful to me and others around me. My old thought process was: "Why am I not enough of a good person, what is wrong with me that you are always late? I need to try harder and not complain because you might never show up at all." The new process will be to talk about this, if it bothers me. Then figure out possible boundaries if nothing changes.

When I take on the feelings of others, I'm hurting from something in the past. My self-worth is getting run over by someone else's self-centeredness, what can I do about this? I used to feel maybe this person is doing this because of something wrong with me. It's not me, it's not you, it's them…Fear was running me over, kicking my ass. It felt that someone wouldn't like me or much less respect and love me.

Prior to my work and changes I didn't value or respect myself enough to set boundaries to protect myself. I've also found that I didn't know how to set boundaries, it was time to learn. I had to learn skills like willingness to end a relationship that is not good for me. Sounds crazy but I had to learn this. There were situations that my relationship might not end but needed to change significantly to make the relationship equitable and respectful. I now make sure and take a hard long look in the mirror about my part in the relationship first, this because I can only work on my part.

## Lesson 30: Feeling big and very small.

It feels like I'm at the intersection of literal and metaphor. I've battled with self-image for as long as I can remember—I'm not the first person who struggled through this. The layers of this are deeper and more complex than most of my emotional baggage. The real beauty of this journey is that anything can change: my image issues are not as big of a deal any longer. I've changed with a lot of work by asking for help; like most people my image issues are grounded in shame and fear. I'm thankful that I have candidly honest and kind people around me that I was able to talk to and be vulnerable around.

Oh boy, do I remember all my conversations feeling really awkward when I was talking about myself in the beginning. My hesitancy to participate in conversations where I was supposed to talk about myself and what was going on where held back and difficult all because of my fear. I found out this fear of expressing my shame was a very significant part of my personality. Lots of work to do with this.

As I started to focus on healthier living, my friend Teela asks me if we could talk. "Of course" I said. To know Teela is always to say yes to her request; she's someone special. She shared how much she cared about me and shared an observation I will never forget. It was that: I'd lost weight and my clothes didn't fit well any longer. She suggested it would be good to get new clothes, even if they didn't feel as comfortable for a while. I will always appreciate her sharing what she thought with me.

When I finally realized whom the updated and current me really was, I figured out the old larger clothes were my ghost image that I was comfortable with; it's what I knew. This image was not accurate and haunted me for years. This revelation helped me see that I was not allowing myself to change, not grow or address some issues. I definitely wasn't fully "present" in the now.

Through my experience I feel that many people today are feeling huge on the outside and so small on the inside. This discourse robs positive energy from the world; I see people carrying this ghost every single day. Sincerely I hope that "Note to Self" helps a person think change can happen. Thank you with all my heart and soul to those who supported, cared and coached me along the way into being me.

## Lesson 31: My half-full glasses.

Was thinking one day about a friend who made me really evaluate the (glass half full) metaphor differently. I asked myself, self—what did I drink out of the glass? How did the first half of this taste feel? Why did I only drink half—all sorts of different perspectives? When I think about the classic adage about a "half-full versus half-empty glass," this equates to expressing and appreciating gratitude. I ask myself: what am I grateful for today, then answer—many, many things.

Some days, situations and moments lend themselves to digging a lot deeper for gratitude and being thankful. Being pissy, ungrateful, unkind or just an asshole never seems to make the situation better nor leaves me feeling like I've made the world a better place with my actions. Conversely for me being positive, thoughtful, and kind 100-out-of-100 times improved the situation and left me feeling better.

> "A half-full glass of kindness always tastes better than a shot of bitterness."
>
> —UNKNOWN

## Lesson 32: It's healthy to feel my feelings.

For me, taking the risk of being vulnerable I've discovered feels far less risky than holding all my craziness inside my mind, body and soul. It's taken feeling my feelings, and raw honesty as I work on myself and being present with my experiences and learning. I've discovered that just making progress is good enough.

This might sound simplistic, but for much of the adult population, vulnerability is both complicated and simple; it's scary as hell and comforting as a warm blanket all in the same breath. When I shut down and don't give myself permission to "feel," I end up carrying these uneasy feelings, which takes up room in my spirit; my emotions get out of whack and body jumps on the bandwagon reacting to this unsettled energy. When I'm able to be comfortable being myself, I connect to those around me in this big old universe. I feel more balanced and positive even in the toughest times. I'm grateful I've learned this.

> *"We cannot selectively numb emotions, when we numb the painful emotions, we also numb the positive emotions."*
>
> —BRENÉ BROWN, THE GIFTS OF IMPERFECTION: LET GO OF WHO YOU THINK YOU'RE SUPPOSED TO BE AND EMBRACE WHO YOU ARE

## Lesson 33: Feelings are real, but not the facts.

I have feelings all day long, everyday, that vary widely from happy, fear, pride, anger, serene and many more. When I experience fear is my physical self in danger? Most of the time I'm not in any danger, it's all in my head. My brain is screaming to protect myself—my heart rate goes up just like being in danger.

For me, the reason I don't say something about how I'm feeling is because I've already scripted out all the negative possibilities: what I will lose, how I will be hurt, the wrong things I will say. Crazy right? No, just a pattern that requires work to change.

This feeling freezes me emotionally and creates walls, which keeps me from growing. My question to myself is why am I feeling _____; then step back for a minute and ask what I'm really feeling, what is going on with myself. If I'm feeling anger then what is unsettled with me; feeling jealousy or humiliation, what is up? Note to Self: look in the mirror for the facts about feelings, they are there. Yes I work on this daily, sometimes minute by minute.

## Lesson 34: Give myself permission to feel my feelings.

Why is crying a good thing? This is a question I've ask myself many times. Then I discovered the simple answer: because holding back whatever I'm feeling is not a good thing.

> *"The stress is always going to come out: someway, somehow and somewhere."*
>
> —Michella Estrada

One of the worst phrases used I feel is "don't cry"; it's alright—let them cry. Encourage people to share and show their feelings, it's good to get it out. Several amazing people I care deeply about are not comfortable crying, they hold back and hold back until they just can't hold it back any longer. I refer to this phenomenon as their "meltdown" when it does finally happen. They know it's coming like a wave, they are all incredibly strong willed people but admittedly struggle with allowing themselves to feel vulnerability. I love them all.

What happens when emotional resistance isn't addressed? I neglect part of my emotional self; many of us do this with one or two issues we're not willing to let go of yet. I've felt neglecting emotions cause more dramatic emotional swings before the dam breaks, then a waterfall everywhere when it does finally happen. Feelings are natural and can be painful and definitely joyful at times. We need all our emotions, keeps the universe and us balanced.

## Lesson 35: Stop managing other people's feelings.

Co-dependency, at its core, is me trying to make other people feel or act a certain way paired with a constant lack of boundaries. Many times this behavior is driven by fear: fear of rejection, fear of confrontation, fear of many things that has caused me to anticipate how someone might act, then I work to avoid that.

I had a friend suggest reading Melanie Beattie's book "Co-dependent No More." it was really my awakening. I was willing to read it, but just didn't know what I was dealing with, so my feelings and actions were all mixed up.

It's fine to be empathic with people, but I can't take on their feelings. It comes down to letting people live their own feelings; I don't need to control it. My codependency came from my need to feel wanted and accepted. This has nothing to do with anyone else but me.

In the past, if someone was feeling bad or good, I took on those feelings. Then I wanted to make myself feel better, which was still about me seeking acceptance. This doesn't sound like the worst thing in the world but if they're not asking for the help, they need to work on their own feelings.

We all have to experience coming to grips with our emotions and feelings. It's an important part of personal growth, who I am and who I am not. Helping, supporting and offering a kind thought to someone and to myself are certainly good attributes. The fine line is giving more of myself than necessary. That is more about filling my own emotional gap than supporting someone and is an unhealthy pattern. To this day, I'm continuing to sort this all out, making progress...not perfection—definitely making progress.

## Lesson 36: Gratitude is grounding.

I've always considered myself a kind and thoughtful person. My reality was that I was outwardly those things but inwardly I was: anxious, distant, unkind and lost.

When I practice being grateful, being full of gratitude, I feel better about the world and myself. It's great, the chemistry of feeling good: physically, emotionally and spiritually. So why is gratitude so fleeting and so easy other times? It felt like I was in a tough place to be grateful and have gratitude. I'm a good actor, so when I first heard the saying "fake it until you make it," it totally rubbed me the wrong way. I later figured out how important it is to go through the motions over and over again—practicing being positive and grateful does make a difference. The turning point came when I wasn't acting any longer, I didn't have to fake it. I was able authentically be grateful.

## Lesson 37: Have to laugh.

A great way to get me "out of self" is something funny; a good laugh opens up my soul for a quick fist-bump with that good feeling that comes with smiling and laughing.

Me in my head about the littlest of things can necessitate the need for laughter to help stop the old patterns of negative thinking. I feel it's important; I love to laugh and I love to be part of others laughing. Please consider being an advocate for cutting-up, but any teasing shouldn't be mean spirited at someone else's expense. It can be cruel and hurtful; it's unnecessary so look at your motives if you do this.

## Lesson 38: Fiercely seek out safe places.

Discovery is powerful; the knowledge we gain and use is in patterns, and patterns are what makes up the universe. Patterns are very difficult to replace, hard even to change. The difficulty stems from me not recognizing what the pattern is, where it came from and how it's affecting you and others. Be relentless about searching for people, places and things that allow you a safe, trusted and inspired place to be the "honest, unfiltered you."

When I found this safe place, I didn't realize how significantly this discovery would affect me. For you it might be a community that you can explore enlightenment and growth in a clumsy, awkward yet trusting way.

My growth takes courage. I didn't start out with much of this but knew that I needed help and couldn't do it myself. The main point was that I started a process with an open mind and lots of willingness which facilitated growth. This happened in part for me because I changed who I was spending time with and the activities I was doing on a daily basis. I was discovering all this is in a safe place with no judgement.

> *"What's fierce? When they talk about "fierceness" what should that really mean? Should it mean that you know how to pout at a camera? Or that you know how to shake your butt? I don't think so. I think fierceness is a raw quality of being vividly present in the act of being alive. You're fierce when you're able to add posi-*

*tive energy to your life and to the lives of people around you! Of course, you should still know how to shake your butt... but that's just called knowing how to shake your butt!"*

—C. JoyBell C., Writer

## Chapter 4

# HOW (Honest, Open, Willing)

W<small>HO SERIOUSLY DOESN'T LOVE AN ACRONYM?</small> Those who would kick a kitty or puppy I'm thinking. H.O.W. is used every single minute in all types of recovery work. Why is it used? It's super simple and easy to remember when worst case things are blowing up and you're melting down. If you're reading these lessons you must be open to change and something different—bravo on that. These lessons are what I've discovered along the way through my lowest point in life.

Being "open" for me was the easiest of the three HOW parts.

"Willing" was the second hardest because it required honesty—of which I was light on in the beginning. I've found willingness without honesty is much like those bubbles kids blow from the bottle—they come in all sizes and look kind of cool but burst and leave a little mess.

Being "honest" with myself has been the hardest part of getting and staying healthy. On this journey of growth, I've found a big part of being honest is holding others and myself accountable.

## Lesson 39: Stop trying fix, just finish and start over.

In my mind when I fix something it means I probably never want to revisit it again unless it's absolutely necessary. Seriously, have a leak, fix a leak...hope the leak never returns again; it's my very linear thought process. When I try to fix feelings, it can be a very fleeting experience and create false hope that the issues don't get revisited. That is not how I'm wired: growth and evolution are not really about being fixed. My growth relies on a journey, not the destination of my choosing. The destination is yet to be determined.

My growth is supported by being candidly honest with myself as much as possible, led by my self-awareness efforts. Action and/or progress equal movement in some way.

## Lesson 40: Make a mistake—start over.

We hear all the time about being more human. Well, here is one more time you will hear it.

I am definitely human—total garden variety. I make mistakes—albeit some bigger than others—but nevertheless, mistakes will always happen. Stacking up all these mistakes can consume a person's entire life. I was that person. Search and find your place and peace in your life, don't carry all that crap around with you. You Matter and the world needs the best you possible.

I've found myself asking questions: How did it really affect people around me? How did it affect me? Where do I need to make amends still for those mistakes so I can move forward with rigorous honesty?

In a nutshell, my first step is willingness with honesty, figuring out why and doing my part to make it right, then forgiving myself and letting it go. I can, have and will start over, continue forward with life, and open up space for something else to enter in my wild and crazy journey.

## Lesson 41: Caring can hurt me sometimes.

It feels like my heart hurts sometimes. It feels like I can't breathe, it's an ache all over. What I have learned, and remind myself regularly, are these feelings are not real physical pain. I've found this to be a great reminder of reality. It's my powerfully fictionalist mind working to make my mind, body and soul into sync.

One of my coping skills is my spiritual routine and fitness. My spirituality can support me staying in balance when the world gets squirrely—and it does frequently. My discomfort feels real; I mean legit-real. We survive this "caring pains," these growing pains with our relationships but it still hurts. Time always supports me when life forces me to grow, albeit confusing, emotional and at times overwhelming; time is my friend.

I feel that given enough time and spiritual work, I will find my way to both ending and starting points of these growing pains about caring.

## Lesson 42: Disappointment is an opportunity for growth.

It is Yin & Yang balance that I can't be happy without sadness. No success will come without failure and lastly courage needs fear. This is how the universe stays in balance; there is no way to short-cut or game the system on this one. It truly does balance. Human nature wants the easiest way, like "I'll take only the good things." I feel this isn't possible or a reasonable way to live my life. It's like I'm trying fixing something versus just being present and living.

I work to keep it balanced, and then when opportunity does present itself, I am open to receive it. I am learning and growing despite my-damn-self at times.

## Lesson 43: I won't keep it, unless I give it away.

Sometimes I wake up bouncing with happy, super peaceful thoughts and proceed to horde all the energy and smiles so I can feel that as long as possible. Well sooner not later those feelings will run out and then I've found they turn on me because I was being selfish with them.

I get transported into the negative "me" space that I've found to be a small and bumping place to live. The negative is necessary, weird to say but necessary to help me appreciate the positive and happiness. I can't love one without learning about the other. Needless to say, happiness isn't a closed loop system that sustains me well at all. I have to share the positive energy to sustain it, with the bigger opportunity being to grow this positivity into all the different forms of joy and serenity.

As I was writing the book, I was thinking about not having anyone to smile at ever again, what a horrible place to be. The emotional and spiritual gap created to never hear the sound of laughter again, wow. I get that aloneness is the next level of awareness but I'm not quite there yet.

Now later, I realized that it's not about what I get back from someone else or from other things. It's about sharing what you have figured out and feel inside is the most important. No expectations for any return on the investment. Just share. My little give to the world is a smile.

## Lesson 44: Feed my creativity.

Feeding and caring of people, plants and the planet is important or all will suffer and eventually die out. Considering this, if I don't feed my creativity, my mind, heart and soul will suffer and eventually could die and be useless.

My mind would go first: not exercising the creative area of my brain will slowly redefine my mind-map. But it's not all doom and gloom; it can be revived and even enhanced with usage. When thinking about various creative skills like music, acting, art, writing and how much they diminish over time, I just wanted to sing, improv, paint and write that second because my creativity is all tied directly to my total being—mind, body and soul.

What goes next is my heart. Have you heard the old phrase: my heart's not in this? When I continually push deeper and deeper into something without any having a passion for it, my mind has tried to protect me and rationalized what makes me happy as if to say, "its not that bad." While working on self-awareness, I've learned to honestly tackle the question about do I love what I'm doing.

Lastly, my soul or spiritual fitness—one might ask why does my soul require creativity to thrive? It's like this: it's a backup parachute—I hope I never use it but when I do, it's got to be ready.

My creativity is always there, it's all within myself and just sits to the side until I am open and create. This is why discovery and self-awareness feeds my mind, body and soul.

*"Creativity is not binary, it's not just a switch you turn on."*

—Doug Shaw

## Lesson 45: Write it down; look at it later.

Years go by and I've hesitated to write down my thoughts. I have an idea, I need to capture it by writing it down. The act of writing it down transforms this idea into something real for me. If I write a list of character defects I would like to let go or write down a list of people I feel I need to make amends with because I've caused them pain in the past—writing this down transforms these bits into tangible and real things for me. It allows me to work on this with actions, make it smaller, and make it bigger with the important point being to work on it. What's crazy, what makes me crazy is my fear, fear that if someone finds these written words how I'm going to be embarrassed, humiliated or ruined. Ruined is pretty dramatic but sometimes it feels like that big of a step in my head. All these damn emotions, past actions, pieces of me I need to work on—yep it gets super real and I need that to happen. If I don't push my discomfort then I won't keep growing.

Me moving past these fears and allowing them to find their way into written word is back to willingness and surrendering to a bigger plan. This might be the simplest, most important and hardest thing I try and do.

## Lesson 46: Happiness is grown.

I've forced a smile, pretty good at it. I've tried to force happy and it just doesn't work that way. Authenticity is the key to a sustainable and interesting life, finding my real self, my truth and being comfortable with wherever I am and with whomever I'm with. This process is really started, continued and grown by finding and understanding the balance of physical, emotional and spiritual fitness (mind, body and soul).

Being joyful and free from my personal limitations involves a lot of work on myself, not on anyone else. This is just another lesson I'm still learning about on a daily basis, truly one day at a time. "I work, I nurture, I learn, I bring into the light my happiness." I've found that fulfillment has to be grown over time.

## Lesson 47: The starting line for healing is feeling.

I've found the more complex my feelings and patterns are the more pain and discomfort will probably be required to uncover what is under the surface. The root cause is the source; it affects my behavior, emotions, thoughts and actions.

Discovery is quite the journey; for me I feel it has been about being open, willing and honest when I look into the mirror. My feelings, specifically my fears, are guide markers to what the hell is going on with me. I answer the question, what is happening around me first, and then the tougher one—what is going on within me? Am I reacting or responding to situations I encounter?

An easy acronym I use as my reference point: HOW (honest, open, willing) am I? It's the only way to grow healthier, evolve into the person that I want to be today. Something I have discovered: what I want myself to be might or might not be my best. I have to be open to what shows up for me as I work on myself.

## Lesson 48: Ask for help.

Many who are exposed to recovery from an addiction are very much aware about the importance and impact of asking for help and being open to helping. It's the foundation for 12-step programs:

1. We admitted we were powerless over some-thing—that our lives had become unmanageable.
2. Came to believe that a Power greater than ourselves could restore us to sanity.

My interpretation: I'm admitting I have a problem—life is spiraling or spiraled out of control and I need to ask for help by surrendering to something bigger than myself. When I started asking for help, there was a necessity to be humble and willing. It became "not about me" because when I ask for help there are actions of surrendering and self-respect. I give myself permission to love myself, so be kind to yourself today.

## Lesson 49: Absolute honesty.

I feel honesty for most people is a common trait; I'm not cynical enough to believe that society, as a whole is dishonest. I will acknowledge there are pockets of people who perpetuate a toxic and unhealthy environment: many of their relationships have negativity associated with them. Definitely people I occasionally offer support to or usually keep my distance from, as they add no value to my life. We all can change, and if they change I might slowly allow them back into my life, very slowly.

To stay balanced I have to be honest with myself; rationaliza-tion to get what I wanted in the past has skewed what honesty actually meant to me. What I've found is telling a well placed half-truth to protect myself or someone else is not going weigh down any relationship.

My experience has proven to me these half-truths are communication based on fear. Dishonesty for me is always the path of least resistance, a fear-based action that is never healthy. I ask myself why can't I be completely honest? I feel I can trust people; I need to remind myself that people will handle as much of the information and truth as they can handle. Just like myself. How much is not for me to decide.

## Lesson 50: The best medicine.

Looking in the mirror provides all sorts of thoughts on mind, body and soul. Being honest and being candid, brutal honesty with myself gets me to the root feeling and into my belief system. I feel very skilled at rationalizing to protect others and myself, but this is about knowing what is right for how I am living in this world. Altering the truth or reality as I see it, is a big no-no.

At times, life feels like it's just too much and too hard to deal with. The overwhelming feeling tells me, this is the best opportunity ever to grow and deal with some things. Fear, ego and pride are the biggest anti-honesty emotions and damn if they're not really strong. Are you being honest with yourself?

I've been told that my negative chatter that rambles around my head tends to be in tip-top shape; when the time is right there is Mr. Negative, nice and loud. Because I've learned this lesson, I have to exercise and workout my coping skills and positive feelings so I'm able to turn fear around when it pops up. It's really hard and never perfect, so just muster up that 5 seconds of courage and do what you have to do. I always feel better when I do.

## Lesson 51: Don't lie.

When history starts to show up in the present, it gets unnerving, makes me anxious at times and puts my fears center stage. All my old questions and many new are right in my-emotional-face.

My friend Alan Schaefer, a current entrepreneur and former rock star, explained his version of measuring his truth in very simple terms: "the tape don't lie." He actually feels so strongly about this message that he shares it with tens of thousands of people each year doing keynote talks. What this simple thought means: I might feel I sound a certain way when I'm singing in the shower or car but if I record myself and listen to my recording, what I hear is an absolute truth. That's some serious feedback and self-awareness.

My spiritual mirror "don't lie" when I'm in the right place to see it. I answer questions from my past in terms of living actions today; I have no interest in repeating the patterns of the past. Don't we all want new, healthier and more positive future patterns? The past is valuable for me because it recounts where I've been. There are answers to questions there; I just have to look hard for them. But the reality for me sometimes is the past is more than I can deal with so I don't. That is just fine; I have to give myself permission to not deal with everything all at once.

## Lesson 52: I can't see inside of a person.

Better communication is absolutely my key to unraveling the mucked up, meddlesome mysteries of the universe. When I ask questions and listen to the answers and truly listen with my heart and head versus just my ears, it's a deeper listen—our other senses collectively are more accurate in hearing what someone is trying to tell us. Think about how anyone can expect to understand how someone is feeling without engaging in a discussion. It's impossible or it's called guessing.

Discussions take on very different forms, the least of which is engaging in an information exchange with people. Creating the story, bottom line, is tricky communication because how you communicate best may very well be how I communicate the worst. Pay attention with all our senses, it will help the world out.

## Chapter 5

# Giving Myself Permission

SO MUCH OF RECOVERING FROM PHYSICAL, emotional and spiritual things is about allowing myself to feel self-forgiveness. When I'm beating myself up over little and big things, I work through a series of thoughts, steps and meditation to respond to the situation. How big should I let this thing get? Is it that important? and what is my part in this? All of the questions and the process I use make me pause and not react with feelings versus facts. Almost always. Without fail, the additional time I've given myself to process affords me a better outcome on what I'm doing.

What I hope I've shared in my message throughout these lessons is mistakes and slips will happen; it's how you respond to these moments that really matters. Be accountable but also be kind to yourself.

### Lesson 53: Yes, I am what I eat.

I've struggled with weight and self-image issues my entire life until a few years ago. A defining moment for me was changing what I was eating. That one change in my life cascaded into a lifestyle awakening. This all started after making a choice to quit eating meat for 30 days, becoming a vegetarian on a challenge from my friend Cat.

What happened was a complete surprise. By changing what I was eating, the surprise was it affected how I consume my food. My relationship with food changed. How, what and why I eat food will never be the same. This challenge laid down by a friend to try something different, challenging my willingness to be open-minded, soon become my anthem toward emotional and physical fitness. Since that day it started, the impact has so profound on my life that I've gone further and focus now on eating vegan as much as absolutely possible, eliminating animal protein completely from my diet.

My commitment to 30 days of no meat, built into my routine a pause button that I was hitting several times a day while I stopped and thought about what I was going to eat. This pause was what I've been missing in my relationship with food. Now it makes more sense of why I'd struggled with my weight and food all these years. No pause for me, I was reacting to emotions using food to cope with life. (*Note that I believe being fit is definitely more than about weight.)

Eating was just happening, I wasn't considering what—or more importantly, how—I was eating. Fairly unhealthy food was filling emotional gaps where I was missing something; it was my survival rope in the absence of healthy coping skills. Fast forward, how I eat today is about how I fuel my body, not how I cope with life. If I'm not intentional about what I'm putting in my body, my body won't react in an intentional way. I am definitely what I eat. Try Vegan— some animals will appreciate it.

## Lesson 54: Being kind is both a lifestyle and attitude.

I've found being a pushover doesn't equal being nice; it's just the opposite in fact. The proverbial doormat syndrome means I don't respect myself enough to say "no" and move on. When I start searching and expecting kindness, it shows up over and over again.

Should I expect kindness before I start being kind to myself? Yes—of course I should and you should—this will always be the answer. I feel the more I respect and love myself the more love and respect show up in my life and flow around me. We are definitely a mirror of our actions, happiness and frustrations—think about it. Living in fear meant attracting fearful people; being insecure and emotionally distant to everyone also meant attracting those types of personalities.

> *Tenderness and kindness are not signs of weakness and despair, but manifestations of strength and resolution.*
> —KAHLIL GIBRAN (1883-1931), LEBANESE AMERICAN ARTIST, POET, AND WRITER

## Lesson 55: Fitness is a lifestyle, not a diet.

One definition of a diet is "a special course of food to which one restricts oneself, either to lose weight or for medical reasons." Fitness, on the other hand, is "the condition of being physically fit and healthy."

So many times over the years I've tried dieting, watching what I eat, monitoring every calorie except the ones I didn't count or cheated. I'm approaching fitness as a whole, as I work on my combination of physical, emotional and spiritual fitness. Losing weight with a diet in lieu of committing to a lifestyle change has proven to be a short-term strategy with no lasting positive health benefits.

Diets have tended to add weight when I stopped starving myself because I resumed my eating habits exactly where I left off when I went on my diet. Making a lifestyle with what I eat such as eating vegetarian meant I had to work on my issues. Becoming a vegetarian forced me to examine how, why and what I consumed for food. This was more about my coping skills and using food as a place to hide from what I felt. I started to address this as I moved into the eating lifestyle change.

I've rarely counted calories or used any diets since embracing a lifestyle change by eating a plant-based vegan diet. I've never been healthier per my Doctor, plus I just feel really good.

## Lesson 56: Vegetables are also fast food.

While writing this book, my second anniversary of my decision to stop eating meat occurred. My friend Cat is a vegetarian and I teased her about not eating meat. She challenged me to try not eating meat or basically to shut-the-#$%!-up with the giving her a hard time because she was tired of hearing about it. She was correct of course. I had no right to hassle her even in jest about her healthy food-lifestyle choice that was important to her as a person. While writing this book, I apologized to her for my lack of initial support and lousy attitude around her healthy personal choices.

Thank goodness she stood up for her beliefs and challenged me. That prompted me to try changing how I eat, one of the single best decisions I've ever made in my life. It enabled me to inadvertently re-wire my relationship with food, which was a major issue.

Behavioral re-wiring is complex and difficult as well, rarely accomplished as an adult. Yes, I can form new habits, new routines, and even change how I approach things but rarely without a serious life-event or therapy does this happen that we can re-wire ourselves. I've now begun a new experience and I am learning about a vegan eating lifestyle—it is hard but worth it.

### Lesson 57: Listen to my own words.

"Note to Self," is a phrase I say to myself and to others as I share what I feel or what I'm thinking. When I "note to self," I'm creating a reference point for something important to me that moment. My advice, my thoughts to others—when do I listen to myself? More than once I've heard myself not taking my own pretty good advice on what to do with a situation.

I'm thinking when I'm discussing it that this is good stuff, then I'm totally not following my own suggestion. WTH, could it be all that different for me. Probably not, I just need to listen to myself. The practice of standing back from what I say, listening to myself and seeing what I think and hear. This type of listening becomes a powerful self-awareness tool when I'm open and in the place to use it. I'd like to use it much more.

### Lesson 58: Love a lot, love often.

My giving and receiving love plus self-loving are all positive actions with amazing outcomes with the realistic risk of rejection and the pain that goes with that. But love is the medicine to be healthier for much of what ails me; it far outweighs the hurt when it doesn't work out so well.

When my mind, body and soul opened up to (receiving) love and giving love—my life changed. I found a path to understanding myself and who I actually was as a person.

I acknowledge terrible things can happen and tough situations come up all the time; they will always happen over a lifetime. Albeit cliché, the adage "what we do in the tough times is our character" is completely true. Less cliché and makes sense is the giving and receiving of love.

Good things and good situations also happen all the time; I just remind myself to enjoy the great moments I have; time doesn't wait on me to be present and participate in life.

We meet many people in our lives, but there are some who influence us for a lifetime. My friend Rebecca Adams Green is one of those people for me; she is my example for love often, love a lot. She left us being loving and selfless, just like I remember her. We miss you.

## Lesson 59: Change: Love myself.

Have you ever had a wave of sadness waterfall over you? If you have then we have something in common. I felt lost at sea and my fears holding my head under water occasionally. When this got so bad that I forgot I mattered and found my self-hatred emotionally and spiritually paralyzing, then I asked for help.

I found myself uttering the words, "I can't take any more and just want to disappear for a little while." I really thought about those words, the meaning and feelings I was living through when that was top-of-mind for me.

At that moment it didn't matter what was going on with me,

something had to change with my life. My only emotion was dread. Has your life ever been at an intersection? This one was not a busy one, it was just a lonely one and I didn't know what to do—so I asked for help.

## Lesson 60: When they zig, I zag.

Doing something different—while life is happening. Life does happen in many ways: I think of this as the "ZIG."

Then when I change it up with a "life pattern," this means that I'm choosing to "ZAG." These little changes are choices supporting a new direction—something different than what I've done in the past.

It comes down to choosing to try something new. Maybe as simple as changing things to change things, do what is unexpected. I choose to try something new, even subtle changes that probably only I notice. What I've found is I have to drive and be accountable for my own change. My actions and responsibility can't live with anyone else. These small changes in my pattern have created feelings of awkwardness and anxiety, but this stretching (my ZAG) definitely supports my evolution.

Many times these life patterns are big, bigger than I feel I'm prepared to deal with at the time. I've found the ability to change these patterns is all about the willingness to ask why. This willingness to admit something is going on with myself opens up my mind.

I've found it hard to initially recognize these opportunities because of the busy lives we lead, the noise that I encounter daily. The more I'm looking for my patterns, the easier it becomes to try changing them.

## Lesson 61: Follow my passion.

The first time I heard the term "unmasking," I really had to think it through. Looking in the mirror and unmasking who I honestly am, for me takes courage and strength.

It's really damn hard and certainly worth it when you get past the initial point of self-awareness. The layers get uncovered when I started focusing on looking at what I saw about myself. It definitely took me being willing to change and then asking for help. A next step was surrendering to something bigger than myself—I call it a higher power, and sometimes I refer to this as God. It depends on the day. For me I don't need to understand why these moments happen, I just need to do the work and take action once it does.

An example I'll share about passion came later in life, I learned this shortly before my Dad passed away. My father wanted to be a coach when he was young. He was a star athlete in every sport—I mean he was really damn good. For him life got in his way; like many others he had to go to work when he was young, so that passion was never revisited, it was basically lost forever. He did find other things like a love of farming, growing and raising things, but the opportunity to live his early passion was never again enjoyed.

When people don't do what they love I feel it leaves the world with mysteries by the million every day—what could have been... Another example is of a dear friend who wanted to be a doctor; she would have been an amazing medical doctor. Again, life happened, her interest and passion was never revisited. My hope is that she does in some way revisit this opportunity; reignite the fire again in some way. The world needs her because she matters and yes it might never happen but if only it could. I empathize and it's easier to say than to do, but talking about it maybe gets it started (again). We all matter; imagine a world with everyone doing what they loved.

## Lesson 62: Being present.

This "being present" was all new information to me, this has been one of the more challenging patterns to change; it required learning some new skills and feeling lots of new things. Maybe it's an art to get in sync with being present? I've been very purposeful about learning and improving this. Being present is directly proportionate to how I feel about self-love, self-worth and myself. As I grow I change. A huge challenge has been "being present with myself"; one would think it's more natural and easier to be present with others, not so much for me.

Not being present equals me being "here" but is really just a checkbox. It means I'm sort-of here but could well be missing or completely not engaged with anything or anyone around me. I am literally emotionally-missing-in-action. If I find myself engaged and listening, then I am making progress. When I'm aware enough to understand if I'm making progress or missing-in-action, I'm actually making progress.

## Lesson 63: Never perfection.

Personal growth is painful, exciting, scary, funny, and imperfect all at the same time. To grow I have to discover and be open to feeling both ends of the emotions: fear and safety, joy and sadness, pride and humility. I forgive myself for the past. At a minimum if I've done the work, I am able to let things go. The work had to be done to make amends to people that I've hurt. All that works is not finished yet; some things takes longer but will need to happen in time.

I'm reminded daily that this all has taken something bigger than myself to help with this clearing of the baggage, of the past. I refer to this as my spiritual investment. I have to make continual progress, always get back up, and always be questioning myself. I just want to make progress in my life. Progress means starting over sometimes, but doing so then moves me forward for the right reasons. Yes, I'm emotionally awkward and clumsy, but taking action and making progress to grow as a person I feel is better than being paralyzed by perfectionism. I've learned perfection does not exist; awkwardness is what makes the world more beautiful than ever before.

## Lesson 64: Things reveal themselves when I'm ready.

I might not feel I'm ready for something to happen but the reality I've discovered is I'm as ready as I need to be when it does. During conversations where opinions differ what are you thinking? Have you ever had found yourself having a conversation where your opinion is starkly different? Do you learn from these moments?

I have been learning lesson after lesson when these conversations happen, starting with revelations about human nature and behavior, myself included. I've found myself thinking how am I reacting to this difference in perspective and why does my opinion differ? These conversations in my head are huge opportunities to think it through and then discuss occasionally.

My awareness increases when I keep my side of the street clean, listen and not try to figure out why the differing opinion makes sense or not while they are still talking. Just listening and discussing is an art and skill: practice, practice. It can be fun once you deal with the internal frustration of not always being right.

## Lesson 65: Relationships can have a shelf life.

My world is constantly changing—me, you, the universe—minute by minute, day by day—it's definitely changing. I grow and evolve; others around me survive and don't seem to care about expanding their mind, body and soul. What others appear to care about is fine, it's "not my circus, not my monkeys."

Not keeping score or judging others is part of how I've chosen to live. I live a different path, my own path, and my own story. In my story there could be friendship, romantic, professional or family relationships. Relationships are born, live and die in movement: they change just like the people involved with them. It does require two of us to make a relationship. I focus much of my movement on the discovery and growth of perspective, beliefs, interests and passions.

When two people don't break a sweat, have willingness to do the work or even acknowledge that changes and growth happens, it makes the relationship difficult, one-sided and unfulfilling. It just doesn't happen over a specific day or suffering, it occurs over and usually includes a lack of honest communication. For me it's been necessary to constantly communicate to grow healthier, feel alive and build on my interesting relationships.

If I'm always putting in more than I get back, it's impossible to continue with a relationship; the relationship will expire. They can have a shelf life and as uncomfortable as ending something can be, it might be time for the end. It's always healthy to keep relationships equitable and balanced; over time it should even out. If not, I need to look at myself and ask why am continuing to invest energy in this.

## Lesson 66: Rinse and repeat.

I've learned that I'm good and bad at routines. When I'm not in a balanced place with my mind, body and soul in my life, then I might have some negative routine that supports a pattern that is negative. I can find myself frequently doing something that isn't consistent in thought with how I want to live my life. When I am in a place of serenity and balance my routines move over to the total healthy side. When I'm not there, I drift and wander into old patterns and routines that I've worked hard to change the frequency of.

Finding what is positive and works then doing it over and over again is good. You can't be at that place forever, but it's all right to be content for a while. Using "rinse and repeat" to my betterment, I sure will. In fact I strive for the positive patterns—good routines.

## Lesson 67: Take a pause.

There are days I wake up and jump right into life; other mornings it requires centering a bit more with meditation and purposeful thoughts. I wish I was perfectly consistent with starting my day, but I'm human, thus flawed, so I give it my best effort.

I've discovered that just acknowledging that I'm thinking about being centered is progress toward self-awareness. Ask yourself, when is a time you can remember using self-awareness? It's an interesting way to think about what is going on inside your head, heart and spirit.

My old self would be comfortable with elements of chaos in my thinking, which for me was never very positive. I would over-think things, project my story and emotions onto situations and people. This is where pausing for a moment and using my self-awareness helps me daily. Not to say I don't still do this—we all do—but I acknowledge what I'm doing or have done. This is one process I use to expand my path for self-discovery. I've found I don't take action on this chaotic type of thinking as often.

## Lesson 68: My areas of resistance.

For years I would not use a recipe when I cooked anything. I attributed this to my independent nature and renegade attitude. Well, I've finally discovered I was straight-up resisting learning how to cook using a largely adopted and proven process known as, following a recipe.

I found myself digging into what my resistance to using something so obvious and simple like a recipe really meant. I had no idea I'd shut down my willingness to learn.

The light went on when a friend made the observation, "It's odd that you say you want to learn to cook using a cookbook but you won't follow a recipe; you're generally so self-aware and open to learning about yourself but not in this situation."

No one was asking me to change political parties or my religion, it was just following a simple recipe. I really wanted to improve my cooking skills. So what was going on with me?

I paused and acknowledged my behavior was odd, then I realized I had bad past experiences cooking. In the past I felt frustrated when I'd ask questions about cooking using a recipe; questions would be met with what felt like impatience at that time.

This is what I remember—perspectives could very well be different; it wouldn't be the first time. Years later, I was still carrying this experience with me. It's nobody's fault, this is about letting go of negative feelings and experiences.

Once I discovered why I was resistant, I worked through letting go of those bad feelings. Sometimes we don't realize why we react or feel a certain way. Today, I'm using recipes and my cooking skills are improving.

## Lesson 69: Respond vs. React.

This is a concept that is not taught in many places. Generally you will not find this topic in the recent issue of HBR, the New Yorker, Wired or even Runners World. If someone brings this (respond vs. react) conversation up we me, I spend time wondering, where does he or she hang out, whom do they hang with? And what's their story to be so enlightened. Weird right? Oh well, it's how I think.

When I look at the dictionary definitions of these words I see they are synonyms, that each has the other in its definition as a verb. So what is the difference? A reaction is basically to act without thinking. I have been taught that a response is a conscious process, that it requires me to consider what I am doing/saying and then to act. The key difference is the reflexive vs. conscious nature of the action. Reactions are great, if you are a soccer goalie or a baseball player! But most human interactions require us to consider and respond.

So why is the distinction important? When I want to live fully I must be conscious, I must be deliberate, I must be engaged. In many ways it is easy to continue to react, but it is far too mechanical, like a needle on a record—it can only do what it has been told to do—follow the tracks laid down in the past. If I want to live a full life I need respond to life.

I often recall an old wise man once telling me "Chemicals react, people respond when they are present to the moment." My friend Randy Roberts shared this lesson.

## Chapter 6

# Self-Awareness

SELF SOUNDS LIKE SUCH A CLINICAL term, psychology mumbo jumbo: news flash for me, it's way more important than all that. It's what I lost somewhere and have been given an opportunity to find because I've learned "my" self is all I have in this lifetime. What helps me continue to grow, be happy and fulfilled is being honest with myself. I feel this honesty is a cornerstone to all the lessons I've shared.

When I wake up and start my day out with some meditation, I've got the mindset to deal with life and all its opportunities plus challenges. This floats my self-awareness right to the top of mind, body and soul. I've found that I can do this meditation anytime, several times and even reset my day. It's all in your power.

## Lesson 70: Bad decisions happen when I'm hungry.

Who hasn't hit the grocery store hungry? The answer is everyone. Generally speaking, I probably wait too long and when buying food happens, I drift from reality and things jump into the basket. I definitely start buying extra things.

If you have completely lost it while shopping hungry and

purchased two of everything, just in case, then we have something in common. That is definitely my crazy deal many, many times over. This is indicative of allowing myself to go too far out of balance. My whole point of sharing this lesson is that everyday life can pretty easily get out of whack and quickly. Is this example life threatening? Probably not, but still out of balance is the gateway to life getting all ridiculous and negative, which results in my serenity being threatened.

Understanding my triggers and doing daily meditation allows my big 3 (physical, emotional, spiritual) balance to work, keeping me centered. I wake up almost every day excited to do these things. It's happily part of my life now.

I look in the mirror; all the emotional mirrors in my life can allow me to honestly see my balance or lack of it. This is an important question I ask myself especially if I feel stuck. Can I look in the mirror? Where are my areas to deal with stress (work, self-image, how I eat, living in the past, grandiose plans for the future)?

## Lesson 71: Hope is tricky.

As I started down my recovery, I heard many people's stories about going from "hopeless to hopeful." So the first time I read Pema Chadron's perspective on why hope is fleeting and basically self-defeating, I didn't understand her perspective. I didn't agree with what she was saying about hope. I read her thoughts over and over again until it finally clicked one day; I understood the bigger message.

Her message was that hopelessness strips away all the past and future from a situation. By stripping away hope from my thoughts and feelings, this allows me to be completely present in the moment. This was a powerful and calming thought process to discover yet very difficult to practice. With practice I am able to let go of what I want, who I was, who I want to be—and "be" in the moment. I don't know the answer to how hope or hopelessness fits into people's lives; it's simple and complicated.

> *"Hope is good breakfast but a bad supper."*
> —Francis Bacon

My experience was that I needed hope early on in my discovery process because I wasn't strong enough to deal with being in the "moment" of what I was feeling. I had not learned enough to understand all the emotions circling in me, much less grasp my complete lack of coping skills for most situations. For me, having hope helped, because I felt really bad with no path out of feeling so disconnected from everything.

The best thing about time is that it changes us if we're open and work on our self-awareness. Hopelessness is still an abstract concept to me but I get that letting go of hope will support my self-awareness and growth by making room to be more present.

## Lesson 72: Eliminate my illusions.

I'm reminded in meditation and reading that other people's reality is not my reality. Life comes at me just as it does you, and checking out feels easier some days. There are even some days that reality feels like a gigantic pill to swallow. I've found it's great to have healthy ways to cope with frustration versus twisting and contorting the situation to fit into my illusion.

The message of my entire book is how my life has improved by finding and consuming information on self-awareness and self-improvement. When I'm self-aware I live in the "no-illusion-zone." My illusions of the past can bubble up to the surface occasionally; it happens. I've discovered self-centeredness is what surfaces most when my illusions are running strong. These situations are where I have to hold an opportunity to hold myself accountable for my action and also forgive myself.

## Lesson 73: Use my tools.

For most of my life, I didn't understand how few coping skills I actually had. Coping skills for me are the tools for living a healthy and serene life.

What I've discovered as I go down my own path to self-discovery are huge gaps in my coping and living skills. As I've worked on myself through self-awareness and self-reflection I'm developing a stronger and more courageous set of emotional and spiritual tools. The emotional tools I am discovering and using require skills to put them into action, and this comes with practice. I get to practice by using them in my daily life.

As life comes at me, the tools for coping with frustration, stress, joy and happiness are growing every day. I'm reminded often by looking at my actions that it's easy to coast and not work on these areas. If I want a good life, I have to keep discovering new things about myself and put my skills into action.

A critical skill I work on is talking about what I'm feeling with people I trust. This has allowed me to get rid of negative feelings, not let them grow and then blow up. Sharing honestly has become something I rely on to live.

Another significant tool I got from one of the 12 steps. It's taking a personal inventory of how I feel and what my actions have been today. Looking at these things—daily or by situation—I feel can be good for everyone. I find it especially valuable and necessary for me to complete every day that ends with a "y."

## Lesson 74: It's not always about me.

As much as my self-centeredness told me the sun orbits around me at times, it doesn't really without causing emotional and spiritual wreckage. I've found that what is going on with you—how you're acting or feeling—probably wasn't caused by me or is even about me. If I feel something that has you unsettled, I can empathize with you, but I have to separate that it still has little to do with me. I can't take away your bad feelings; that is up to you. In the past I've projected on people what I thought they might feel and why, then I internalized this as something I did.

Here is how I'm working through this "me" issue:

1. First, I have to think it through and meditate about it. This is taking my personal inventory: how I feel, what I've done, why I feel that way and do I need to make amends to anyone.

2. I must share what I'm feeling with someone. It needs to be someone I trust; it could be conversation via text, Facebook message, phone or even in person.

3. Lastly, just asking myself questions like "what is really going on" and "am I reacting or respond-

ing to the situation" usually provide me enough clarity to handle things.

My understanding of what I see in the mirror is embracing self-awareness. I keep looking into the mirror to figure out what is going on, and then try to make changes. I feel the world doesn't function well with just me; I've found it takes "we."

## Lesson 75: My fitness.

When I'm figuratively carrying around unaddressed issues— and we all do—then I feel weighted down on the inside, not very emotionally fit. Life serves up all sorts of things: it's difficult to know if people are struggling unless they tell you. Internal emotional pain is complicated but can be addressed by working on it, lots of work. There are cases that the work may include seeing professionals and takes medication; whatever it takes to feel better and have a life you enjoy living.

Working on my inside are emotions that require a similar type of commitment as my outside. When I reflect back I've changed my outside many times, lost and gained over 1,000 pounds in all my efforts, but I'm always changing. Outside was fit at different points in time but my inside was rocky and unhealthy: they are connected. One can't last long without the other being healthy.

When I'm happy and peaceful on the inside, it feels easier to maintain a happier outside. The "light shines" as they say; everyone can see it a mile away in my spirit and most evidently in my actions. I feel good about life and myself most of the time these days because I am doing the work on "me."

## Lesson 76: Don't look back.

There are a few baseball people who are legendary for their famous quotes. Yogi Berra and Casey Stengel are famous for their malapropisms, sage observations coupled with wry humor, intentional or not.

Commenting on a bad situation, Berra once said, "It's like déjà vu all over again."

Regarding life, Stengel observed "There comes a time in every man's life, and I've had plenty of them." My life has been like that lately. I've been working on making a career transition. I have a great job, but it isn't located where my family wants to live. In order to live where I want to live, I needed to find a way to earn a living that was 600 miles away from the job I love.

I created a plan. I worked the plan, identifying several alternatives to the current job, including a significant HR consulting opportunity and another opportunity working in a social media agency. I embraced these opportunities and then went to speak to my employer, telling them it was time for me to move on. They surprised the hell out of me by offering me the opportunity to become a virtual manager, working from home and managing a staff from afar.

I was ecstatic. I called the consulting company and told them I wouldn't be starting after all. I quit the part-time social media gig I was doing in the evenings. I prepared to move into the new virtual work assignment. And then the phone rang. It was someone wanting to interview me for another opportunity. I accepted a new job and told my boss yet again, it's time for me to move on.

Legendary pitcher Satchel Paige is famous for saying, "Don't look back. Something might be gaining on you." He's right; you need to keep looking ahead. That's the way you'll find the next opportunity. My friend Mike Vandervort shared this lesson.

## Lesson 77: The many small things that make big differences.

Among many things, I am a proud son, and a believer that my best work often comes from simple, frequent interactions and encouragements—small things that make big differences.

I remember being at my Dad's retirement party twenty years ago. The place was packed and Dad gave a thank you speech saying said he would miss the people but not the work. Lots of people spoke to me that evening and told me tales of the little things Dad did over the years that strengthened their connection with him. Straight talking, saying thank you and not taking himself too seriously were all in the mix.

When he died, I had the tearful honor of reading the eulogy at his funeral. Once again the place was packed, this time with people he knew from his childhood, his school days, his national service, his long career and his long, but not long enough, retirement.

So many people, so many connections, reaching almost all the way back through 76 years of life. I spoke to many people that day and was overwhelmed by the many small things he did that helped so many networks connect and thrive.

He was an effective friend, campaigner and lobbyist, and he did it old school—visiting people, sending letters, making phone calls. Lots and lots of little things that, across his community, made big differences. My friend Doug Shaw shared this lesson.

## Lesson 78: Vulnerability is powerful.

Where does vulnerability fit in with fear and anger? I feel being vulnerable is the complete opposite of fear and anger. Sharing what I'm feeling opens me up to the world. Stating that yes, I am filled with fear definitely makes me vulnerable; I might even lose something—a job, a love, or friends—with my vulnerability but it all makes me stronger.

Talking about what bothers or concerns me opens up space for me to feel. Part of discovering how to feel means surrendering my ego and pride and letting go of the fear; my willingness to open up space for my spirit happens and I get to experience and grow. Many times surrendering feels like vulnerability because it is new and unknown.

## Lesson 79: Best efforts yield both failure and success.

I can try and try at something with my best effort and fail completely. Then I also try and try, do my best and the effort delivers a smashing success. Trying and quitting are both taking action...this is about movement, about effort, again about taking action. Just by doing or taking action on something, I experience movement in my life. I gain experience and more knowledge that yields growth. It's the inaction—the say a lot but never "do" a lot— that will bury you in self. This isn't good. It's hard to see when it's happening but in reflection I'm gaining something from every success and failure.

I've met people who work their whole lives to never fail, not make a mistake and live the no-risk life. Ultimately this extreme effort ends up being their failure because they never take chances, never experience unknowns and live a half life.

I am discovering how to be intentional with my thoughts and actions every single day. I've experienced amazing outcomes in life from my focus on making being intentional automatic. No matter where the end of the story lands, success or failure, the journey is about growth, perspective and enjoying my life.

## Lesson 80: Feed my spirit.

It happened: I finally became aware that I have to feed, not starve my spirit. I have to contribute the best things possible, much like anything I've wanted to change and expand. When I tried out being vegetarian, it was about changing my eating habits and behavior. The spirit is no different; I've changed my quiet times and feed my spirit by being more intentional and positive. For me, the spiritual experience is acknowledging there is something bigger in my life than just myself. I believe my spirit shows up and exist in all my actions, deeds and thoughts.

I have variety of references in my spiritual experience: my higher power, God, and the universe. The God of my understanding—however I refer to this—created a sense of humor, so I'm assuming (s)he gets the situation and the context I choose to address conversation.

My cornerstone of spiritual fitness starts every day with meditation. I get centered and remind myself of my purpose. I've found that not starting my day this way makes for more chaos and reactions. My spiritual journey is the simplest and most complex area of my self-awareness. The tug of war in my mind and heart from old patterns and behaviors are real and realistically part of my hard-wiring, which is so damn hard to change, if not impossible.

All this might sound hippyish and new agey but I feel they have this right. So let's burn some incense and get "right" with your fantastic day. Meditation happens to be my drug of choice; bonus that it's both legal and free. Feeding my spirit so it's nice and fit takes a commitment; it's no different than exercising to be physically fit.

A side note: I found it poetic that when editing this lesson I was completely thinking of two amazing organizations: Share Our Strength, founded by Debbie and Billy Shore (www.nokidhungry. org) and St. Jude Children's Research Hospital founded by the late Danny Thomas (http://www.stjude.org/history). Be sure to check them out.

## Lesson 81: Emotionally bankrupt.

The day I stopped drinking, I start feeling and I was surprised how quickly a tidal wave of emotions hit me when I stopped feeling so disconnected and spiritually numb. I found myself feeling all my feelings from years of them being tucked deep away in places I couldn't find. I'd think, "I have no control over what I'm feeling, I hope this is a good thing." Now, with lots of work on my mind, body and soul I'm very grateful to be present when I'm feeling emotion, no matter what those feelings may be.

It's fairly easy for me, almost automatic to share kindness. I am less versed on sharing "grounded gratitude" which I've discovered to be a deeper more engaged type of gratitude and kindness. Grounded gratitude is equal parts humility and gratitude. I didn't have a clue what the real meaning of this meant for years, but I started to be willing and open to learn.

Once this happened my life changed, and I started experiencing genuinely humble feelings. It felt like I started with very little emotional equity when I was learning how to "feel my feelings." This journey has also taught me about sadness and pain; these are part of what we all have to experience to grow.

## Lesson 82: Sometimes an invisible boat is the only way to get there.

A man and woman walk up to the shore, the woman was telling the man how she had lived an incredible life but not without much pain, growth and work to get to an incredible life. He was very interested because he was living the opposite of an incredible life: life sucked. He was carrying around lots of negative emotions, experiences and thoughts but was at the point he wanted to change.

The woman pointed and said "ok, see that big decadent cruise ship over there?" He said yes. "Looks very nice." She said, "Do you see the small but water-ready boat over there with only one person in it?" He said, "No, I see a person standing in the water but no boat." The woman exclaimed, "You need to get on the boat to get over the island where serenity and happiness will be." The man retorted, "There is no boat, just a person in the water." The man was more comfortable going on the nice looking and decadent cruise ship. The woman asked the man again, "Are you ready to be happy and have a more fulfilling life?" Yes, he replied. "I'm ready, I can't take it anymore." The woman stated, "Well go get into the boat with that other person!"

In my life, my best thinking, my best efforts got me to the point of unhappiness, emptiness, and walking through a life I didn't understand or enjoy. I needed to believe in something bigger than myself to understand how I live a life I enjoy.

To finish the story; the man made a choice to take the little crappy boat, not the gorgeous cruise ship. The cruise ship left the shore, made it halfway to the island and stopped, turned around and came back. "That's as far as it will go," said the woman. The cruise ship represents a life full of grandiose, promises, and self-centeredness but never taking action.

The man went over to the person in the water and asked, "Where is the boat"? The person in the boat handed him an invisible paddle. The person with a smile said, "Now paddling, that's up to you."

The man stopped thinking about it and started paddling; when he had faith in something bigger than himself, the boat appeared to him. The paddle and the boat represented surrendering his will. A suggested action like having faith in something you can't see supported him building the tools to have that incredible life.

## Lesson 83: Being spiritual.

Being a spiritual guy was not on my radar but faith and trust are now threads in my tapestry every single day. They are interwoven with all the rest of my life; now I feel more grounded in loving, gratitude and my self-respect. I felt I needed filters, pauses and conditions when I am giving and receiving of loving feelings. In that survival mode we have, I had built limits and conditions to protect myself on how much I can love others and be loved, so I wouldn't be hurt.

It was a long, winding and frightening path to see what I was doing to everyone I care about and myself. I've found being spiritual is an important part of my daily routine and staying healthy. It is about being self-aware and self-discovering the why of what is happening to me and around me. There are times when the why is not obvious and takes a lot of work to figure out all the pieces, then discover where those pieces go. Thank goodness I am at this place today that I figure things out sooner or later anyhow. I hope you arrive here someday with me. The light will always be on friends.

## Lesson 84: Pillow talk.

Pssst. What is between you and me, stays between you and me.

## Lesson 85: Surprise me.

My friend likes to go to her favorite craft cocktail place named Valkyrie in Tulsa, Oklahoma. Over a couple of years, the staff gets to know her, her personality and drink likes and dislikes. Picture this—she sits down, they ask "what she's in the mood for today?" She tells them, "Surprise me." Over time, a level of trust has been established. She shared, "I've got to know them, they have a great understanding of mixology, I like their style and their sense of adventure—it has an excellent quality to it." There are many different ways this concept works and all are awesome.

This is about building relationships: positive relationships are built on trust, enjoyment and communication. This is a great metaphor for life. Living in the moment and being present is all about trust. I work to trust whatever the universe "surprises me" with albeit possibly new and quite different. I've found it will be exactly what I needed at that point in time. I give myself permission for the universe to take me some place I don't know anything about. Got to believe.

Chapter 7

# Lessons Learned

I FEEL THINGS CAN BE REPLACED. I lost my wallet while writing this part of the book, and yes, it presented a hassle for several people besides me. The loss separated me from something I carried with me for several years: a piece of paper. I wrote something down, a reminder of my commitment to change, when I very first stopped drinking. As I think about this being gone, I've found what is important was not the actual thing; it's the spirit and intent of the message. The message helped remind me what I committed to early on when I was so lost and in pain. I committed to doing whatever it takes to get healthy and not drink. I didn't look at it very often as the years passed from when I wrote it; I saw it usually when I grabbed a credit card to pay for something.

When I revisit the beginning of my journey to change into someone who is focused on self-awareness, I go back through the words and messages I've heard and read. I remind myself not to judge my own worthiness to share, but to share what I've discovered and used to make my life better.

I feel it's important I share what helps me each day, just in case it might help someone else. There are many great organizations and people in this world, and I wanted to share one of my favorites: Southwest Airlines, who after 6 weeks returned my wallet with everything still intact that someone had turned into them. Thank you.

## Lesson 86: Willingness.

It was one of those days when a friend shared this thought with me: "You are being a selfish asshole if you don't ask for help from the people who care about you." Those who don't ask for help are self-imposing themselves to an island that gets very dark and endless: no stopping, no starting, just drifting. I've been to that island; it feels real and it sucks. I didn't understand what I needed—more importantly, I didn't know what asking for help looked or felt like. I finally arrived at a place where asking for help seemed to be the only choice; why this happened I do not know.

Asking for help today is because I love and respect myself. My goal is not to be a self-centered asshole. I remind myself that I might be helping someone when I ask him or her for help. Willingness is the key. It's a money-back guarantee to return to the lousy place you were if you don't like being willing to change. Please try it.

## Lesson 87: Find my voice.

I'm an advocate for finding whatever helps you need to sort out life and to get you closer to happiness. I've used professionals to help sort out feelings and issues. One told me...I need "you need to find your voice." It was a profound conversation, changed my life. I will never forget it. We discussed what that meant. My voice was in the background with others and myself. Fear had been in my way: a wall of why I wouldn't talk, stand-up for myself and state my honest feelings. The new goal was to push through my fears. What would really happen if I said what I really wanted to say with a situation or relationship? Nothing dangerous, someone might get mad and maybe leave but likely talking with some occasional yelling. I learned that day how someone else feels are not my feelings and can't dictate my actions, I can't and shouldn't try and be both sides of any conversation. Say what is on my mind, say what I'm feeling: this is how I found my voice. I am constantly discovering new parts of my voice, I'm hopeful you will find yours.

> *"Don't try to figure out what other people want to hear from you; figure out what you have to say. It's the one and only thing you have to offer."*
>
> —BARBARA KINGSOLVER, AUTHOR AND POET

## Lesson 88: Sense of self.

Early in my life I made a decision to be a different person than my father. Yes, there were lots of reasons, and all of them made sense at that point in time. I was very committed to being different from him. I'm not here to profess this was the right or wrong thing to do; I can't change it so I'm learning from my retrospection.

What I've discovered is that working so hard to be different from someone left my own self-my truth a little blurry. My sense of self was tied up in trying to NOT be like my father, instead of discovering what my own true identity was, independent of him. Today, I realize this has nothing to do with my Dad, who actually passed away while I was writing this book. I know that he did the best he could when he was doing it. I love him and miss his laughter.

My being unsettled and searching for my sense of self always left me trying to recreate myself. Just being myself wasn't an option. For those raising children: be honest, be open and communicate with them, teach them what being independent and their own person is all about. Ask yourself a few questions: Who am I? What am I passionate about in life? What was I passionate about when I was younger?

> *"Turning pro is a decision. But it's such a monumental, life-overturning decision (and one that is usually made only in the face of overwhelming fear) that the moment is frequently accompanied by powerful drama and emotion."*
>
> —FROM TURNING PRO BY STEVEN PRESSFIELD,
> AUTHOR

My decision moment was when I acknowledged something had to change with my life. There was no flash of white light. I knew it was time to change; it was definitely monumental and absolutely life overturning. Since that decision it's been an ongoing process that shouldn't ever stop—a process that is painful, joyful, confusing and enlightening. My very first step at finding my truth was willingness—willingness to admit I have some problems, big ones.

## Lesson 89: I can always reset my day.

I am in control of how I feel and how my day goes. Who hasn't woken up feeling a bit off and then slid into a bad mood for the day? I didn't know why but I definitely knew I was not in a positive head or heart space. I can simply hit the reset button and just start over my day. Yep, just repeat after me... I'm starting the day over right now. Repeat: Let it go; start over. Let it all go; start over. Live with no apologies, it's a new day.

The most challenging piece of this lesson is being aware that I'm slipping into that bad mood or negative, darker place. Spot checking my mood, my attitude and myself is always a good preventative action for me.

## Lesson 90: Jealousy.

My grandmother once told me, "My sister is one of the most jealous people in the world. I know this because I don't have a jealous bone in my body, but I can see it in people."

"Okay, Gramma. Of course you're not the jealous type. Not. At. All."

I still laugh when I think of that conversation. We hate the things we see in other people that remind us of ourselves. And jealousy and envy are some of the worst qualities in the world, which sucks because I am a jealous and envious person:

Career envy. Money envy. Running envy. Height envy. Weight envy. Hair envy. Shoe envy. Spouse envy. Dog envy. Baby envy. Location envy. Hotel envy. Eyebrow envy. Zip code envy. Beach house envy. Lifestyle envy. Upgrade envy. Good towel envy. Nice sheets envy. Landscape envy. Paint envy. Furniture envy. Jewelry envy. Socks envy.

This is tough to admit. My life is great—and I don't lack for a single thing—but I sometimes wonder how and why people are doing better. Then I find a way to knock it down.

"You work harder than me? You are smarter than me? Well, you know what? Your face is stupid."

Ugh. So bad. So awful. So human. And your face is fine.

Jealousy and envy are more about insecurity than anything else. We have a void in our lives—one that we probably caused—and we deal with our void by attacking someone else instead of coming to terms with our own personal or professional failures.

Or we don't have a void and our brains are broken.

So how do you solve the problem of being jealous or envious of another human being? Heck if I know. I think I am much better, these days, because I am honest about it. I try to remember that I can be happy for someone while struggling with issues in my life.

You like your family? Oh how fabulous for you. Why don't you go fuck yourself, I mean, go ahead and have a healthy relationship with your parents. That is great. I'll be over here—not being jealous—figuring my shit out.

Jealousy and envy are unnecessary causes of suffering and anguish in our lives. And those dysfunctional behaviors—even if never publicly expressed—make us stupid, petty and unlikable.

If you catch yourself feeling jealousy or being envious of another person's success, give yourself a little grace but please try to stop those behaviors ASAP. It's a waste of time. Wish my Gramma had realized that in her lifetime. My friend Laurie Ruettiman shared this lesson.

## Lesson 91: Lose my willingness; I've lost my way. Turn around.

The secret ingredient for continuing to grow during change, dealing with loss, evolving through growth, seizing the moment is "willingness." If I'm willing to listen, learn, be accountable, hold people accountable, forgive, love, be humble and compassionate, trust, surrender, embrace something bigger than myself, check my pride and ego, then I'm on track with willingness. Only doing one of those things gets you pointed in the right direction with being willing.

If I lose my willingness then I'm lost. I've found I regress to behaviors and thoughts from the old me, the one I struggled to respect. The lack of willingness to change creates a mind, body and soul silo that I feel stops growth dead in its tracks, a complete dead-end.

My secret ingredient #2 is "the Reset." I am able to reset my day at any moment; it's all up to me. Only I have the choice and power to reset which takes being willing, willing to accept my part, willing to take action to change my day and situation.

Starting over isn't a failure; it's a smarter beginning. I felt it starts another journey or adventure. Willingness and the "Reset" are the some of the keys to my serenity.

## Lesson 92: Taking action.

I was visiting my friend Chris a few years ago and started complaining that I just don't like doing laundry. Yes, first world problems, I admit it. Then my friend has the nerve to offer me help: "C'mon let's go do that laundry." This was a lesson in taking action, a big lesson I learned about myself. I reflected on why I so resistant and procrastinated on doing a fairly easy task. My procrastination was taking up energy and space, especially because I was thinking about washing clothes versus being present with my friend.

Laundry is one thing in life I don't tend procrastinate. My friend's caring voice echoes loudly with me when things need to get done. Have people in your life who care enough to be honest with you.

Tips to myself about taking action:

1. Do something, then mark it off your list. It feels good.

2. Don't let your thoughts about what you're doing weigh down and slow down what you're doing. Is overthinking it better than overdoing?

3. Don't promise it will happen in an hour. Don't mail something tomorrow. Either get it done or say no you won't do it or explain the list of things you're required to complete before it gets done.

4. Life with action is art that speaks to someone—it's movement and evolves into infinite opportunities.

5. Sometimes getting things done is really difficult. Stay positive, communicate what is going on and try to make progress.

## Lesson 93: Be of service.

Early in sobriety they tell you over and over again at least two things: "don't use" and "be of service." I've heard hundreds of times to show up early and leave late, to help do something that is serving someone else but yourself.

This isn't only a great suggestion for someone trying to change their life; it's bigger than that. It is about being selfless in your thoughts and actions. Both professionally and personally I've discovered life has a different tone when I'm helping someone else out. It feels good; the world could be a better place by me helping out with something, which is not for me to decide or declare.

I've felt the suggestion to be of service to others when you're trying to stop drinking was about giving me a break from thinking for a few minutes. Service to others looked like taking out the trash, dumping ashtrays, setting up chairs and making coffee. I've got very fond memories of the comfort that provided when I didn't know anyone—specifically didn't know myself and was so uncomfortable with life. Think about volunteering in some way and see how it goes.

## Lesson 94: Look up, it's magical.

I've taken hundreds of trips on business and traveled to lots of places. Most of the time, I admittedly never looked up and around to see what the wonderful world had to offer. I so limited my experience to what was right in front of me. Some might say, "he was focused," but no, that was not it. I was just bouncing through life getting the day or trip done as best I could but definitely not living an awesome life, experiencing experiences.

I'm not carrying any regrets about never taking time to experience all the things that were available. I feel I know what counts now that I'm more self-aware so I work to experience places and things now. It's important for me to be present, reminding myself to pause, slow down or even back up and look around.

Time will never happen again. It's unique, so I work on being intentional. Tonight I will look up: is there a moon or stars or wind blowing in the trees? If I really pay attention there might even be a *gustnado to watch. (*I learned that term writing this book. Look it up.)

## Lesson 95: Advocacy. Make it a priority.

It's always interesting to observe how uncomfortable conversations are where people are pretending to listen to be sort of polite. I remember doing just that, pretending. It wasn't honest or polite and I was secretly wishing I had an invisibility cloak (movie reference) to slip out of the blah, blah, blah conversation. It's the truth, it happens, but that doesn't make it the right thing to do.

Even being a little dishonest can send me down a path where I go the easiest route, which adds zero value to my life or others. No one is perfect, I'm not perfect; I'm being a little lazy, coasting in life a bit when shortcuts like not being present in conversations happen often. Either way, I've lost sight of an important priority in my life when this happens.

I subscribe to being an advocate of being intentional. I've had to find and develop my own voice, which helps me participate in these conversations I found boring and not engaging before. Everyone needs to find their voice; encourage people to be a contributor, a participant in their own life.

What is going on with your life right now? I suggest recording your thoughts in some way and refer back to them. This allows you to be present with your own conversation.

## Lesson 96: Exercising my spirit builds strength.

I first started my journey to a healthier and more fulfilling life because I was unhappy and felt empty. The journey started out of necessity because the pain had gotten bad enough, quite intolerable. Something had to change—that something ended up being me.

I've discovered that I had no idea my spirit was all right in some ways and very broken and confused in others. I started working on my issues by first admitting I had a problem, with my highest priority being that I was changing how I felt by drinking to much. I've found that my issues were only a symptom of a bigger problem, which for me was "me." I was the issue. Trying to change the way I felt with unhealthy means got me further from living a life I could enjoy, a vicious cycle many people are finding themselves in.

I started by exploring all the definitions of spirituality and what it didn't have to be for me. Discovering what I couldn't see isn't the easiest of things to do from point A to point B; it moves around a bit more than that. I quickly realized I had to practice being spiritual to understand my spirit more. My view that being kind is good enough to be spiritual for me was not working out; there is more to it than just being kind to others.

Spirituality gets called many different things: the light, energy, higher power, something bigger, the force, God, Buddha, Christ, the Universe and many more. For me it's God and my higher power, those are my conversations. Investing time discovering what spirituality looks like to different people I feel is time well spent. It might turn out to be one of your favorite areas to explore.

## Lesson 97: Serenity.

Over the last few years I've discovered serenity, inner calm and peace—thank goodness, as I needed them all. People, places and things impact me far less as I'm doing the work to maintain and grow my physical, emotional and spiritual fitness. Perfection never happens—some days something might get to me, other days it all bounces off me. Discovering serenity is definitely part of the growth process.

A good check-in for me is how rattled I get about someone that has really very little to do with me directly. For the longest time, I didn't have self-awareness or emotional tools to let things go. Letting things go for me was extremely difficult at times. A great example: a comment by someone runs through my head on what I did, a hundred times. The outcome of this chaos mind chatter is typically negative, so I need to make it stop. I call this scripting— it's my internal conversation with myself and it's driven by my fears and my self-centeredness. I've worked hard to stop this process and feel I've made significant progress, but it will never be perfect. That's all right, today I have more room for love, quiet and serenity.

## Lesson 98: Sharing helps me keep small things small.

Opening up and sharing with strangers in groups and meetings has taught me to not be in control. Do I share every single thing that comes to mind? Of course not, I need to feel safe enough to share in order to open up about what is going on with me.

Does sharing and willingness get easier for me over time?

Yes it does. I still practice sharing all the time and think about it frequently because it's important to me. It's not automatic for me yet but with continued work and growth, maybe someday.

When I share, it could be about a comment someone made about my work or someone thought my sense of humor was weird or patronizingly questioned my decision about eating vegan. I work to find a way to share so I'm not keeping all that emotion on the inside. With more discovery and work, I've been able to change and grow—now I tend to share more quickly and more often. It feels good to verbalize that something is bothering me and the reasons why.

The sharing helps me usually determine my issues; at least I feel my questioning how I feel it puts some context to the situation. Most things that bother me are small, to keep them small takes some work, simple work—it's way easier to let go and move on to the important things in life.

## Lesson 99: We're all in this together.

I suggest we shouldn't live in isolation; let's work this out together. Please consider sharing your thoughts with me. I would love to hear from you about your "Note to Self" lesson. Share your lesson at the website address below, or tweet me with #notetoself99. Thank you.

www.bryanwempen.com/notetoself99
@bryanwempen

Very Kindly,
*Bryan Wempen*

# Additional Ramblings

1. We all struggle. I struggle with various things in life. I've concluded the struggle—the challenge—presents an opportunity to grow and heal.

2. My friend John Sumser shared a thought with a mutual friend recently that really spoke to me: Sad is what healing feels like. "Don't be in a hurry to be done with sad. Wait until it is done with you. It's okay if that takes a while."

3. Find a refuge, a mountain top, a room that is only yours, a redwood path, a place to rest where you can have a conversation with life.

4. When you and I judge people, places and situations, quickly stop and think—I don't know their story.

5. Learn to say no and not feel too bad about it.

6. Just by questioning why you did or felt something, you're growing.

7. Be kind to yourself today.

8. Don't be selfish, there are people who care and want to listen.

9. Find something to laugh about, it should be mandatory.